NEWTON: THE LIBERATOR

By the same author:

Newton
The Liberator

John Pollock

KINGSWAY PUBLICATIONS
EASTBOURNE

First published by Hodder & Stoughton 1981
Published in the USA by Harper & Row 1982
Published by Lion 1996
This edition by Kingsway 2000
Reprinted 2003

ISBN 0 85476 884 X

Published by
KINGSWAY COMMUNICATIONS LTD
Lottbridge Drove, Eastbourne BN23 6NT, England.
Email: books@kingsway.co.uk

Book design and production for the publishers by
Bookprint Creative Services, P.O. Box 827, BN21 3YJ, England.
Printed in Great Britain.

For T.W. and Grady

Acknowledgments

Fuller details were given in the first edition, published as *Amazing Grace: The Life of John Newton*, but I would like to express again my thanks to the following for permission to use copyright material: the late Miss Catherine Bull; the Cowper-Newton Museum at Olney; Ridley Hall, Cambridge; Dr William's Library, London.

I am grateful also to the Revd Francis Dufton, the Revd Robin Leaver, the Revd John M. Preston, Dr John Wesley White, and Mrs J. E. Williams who typed my manuscript with her usual skill; also the staff of the London Library and the National Maritime Museum.

Finally I would like to mention my late father-in-law, Sir Richard Barrett-Lennard, Bt., who gave me much encouragement but died before publication. Newton's boyhood home in Essex was a tenant farm on the Belhus Estate of Sir Richard's ancestors. He lived at Belhus himself before the Second World War, and this makes a pleasant link between subject and author.

John Pollock, 2000

Amazing grace (how sweet the sound)
    That saved a wretch like me!
I once was lost, but now am found,
    Was blind, but now I see.

'Twas grace that taught my heart to fear,
    And grace my fears relieved.
How precious did that grace appear
    The hour I first believed.

Through many dangers, toils and snares,
    I have already come;
'Tis grace hath brought me safe thus far,
    And grace will lead me home.

Contents

Prologue

Amazing grace, how sweet the sound . . . The great hymn was not yet written or even in his mind, early that wild autumn evening. A strong wind was rising to a gale. John Newton struggled in the fading winter daylight from his parish church of Olney in the English Midlands towards his vicarage. He turned up the short drive, pushed open the door and threw off his cloak and sea captain's jacket.

Pausing at the parlour to blow a kiss to his dearest Polly he hurried into his study. The mid-week prayer meeting must start within a few hours at the Great House and he had not yet written a new hymn. Each week he liked to introduce a fresh one, set to a familiar tune. Some, he knew, were mere jingles of praise or teaching, but others were being sung up and down the land, in these years of the 1770s.

The little study was warm. Polly always made sure that the maid lit a fire early; Newton poked it, threw on more logs and settled at his desk. Rain beat on the windows and the wind rattled the glass as he turned the pages of his wellworn Bible, looking for a theme. He had been reading the story of King David and took it up where God promises to establish the House of David for ever; and David, overwhelmed, turns to prayer. Newton's eye lighted on the words: 'Who am I, O Lord God, and what is my house, that thou hast brought me hitherto?'

Who am I? David, the poor shepherd boy, the exile, had become a mighty king; David the sinner had been forgiven and from his line would be born Jesus the Saviour of the world. And John Newton held the overwhelming privilege

11

of preaching this Jesus among the people. But, *Who am I?* Who am *I?* Newton the exile, the servant of slaves; Newton the rebel and atheist, the proud, violent blasphemer.

The gale rose higher. He could hear the roar as it shook the trees in the garden. He could feel the wind which found a way through the window and under the door. Newton shivered. He moved to the easy chair near the fire, and mentally pursued the theme of the wonder of God's grace which had saved a wretch like him. He looked back at the amazing coincidences which had played their part. He recalled as equally amazing his love for a girl he could hardly expect to win, which had burned unquenched through his misfortunes and his fornications.

He closed his eyes. The howl of the wind, the splash of the rain could not fail to remind him of another gale, far out to sea in the North Atlantic, when he was a young man of twenty-two, the storm on which his entire life hinged. His mind began to recapture the memory, his heart to swell in gratitude. His ears grew deaf, his head nodded. Imperceptibly he slipped into a vivid cat-nap dream, reliving that dreadful moment when a great sea shook the *Greyhound* from stem to stern, in the early hours of 10 March 1748, and water began to flood the cabin and he heard a cry, 'We are sinking!'

'*We are sinking!*' Young Newton leapt from his bunk and without pausing to pull on thicker garments against the cold he rushed towards the companion hatch to give help on deck. The captain called down for a knife. As Newton ran back to fetch it another of the ship's company dashed up the companion ladder, and was swept overboard by a wave.

Newton found the knife and came on deck. He judged at once, from his years of experience in the merchant marine and the navy, that the ship might sink at any moment. A wave had torn away the upper timbers on one side so that she filled fast. The hull was weak after eighteen months in the tropics, and the *Greyhound* would have sunk already had she been carrying a Slave Trade cargo.

The ship tossed and rolled. Newton struggled in the darkness to one of the pumps and joined another man pumping hard, while others bailed with buckets, or tore up clothes to help staunch the leaks. When day broke and they found themselves still alive, Newton called out cheerfully above the wind as he pumped, 'In a few days this distress will serve us to talk of, over a glass of wine!'

'No!' said his mate. His tone was grave. 'It's too late now.' He was preparing to die.

Newton laughed. Hour after hour he worked at the pumps, his teeth chattering with cold despite the exertion, his strength weakening as their efforts seemed hardly to postpone the *Greyhound*'s almost inevitable foundering. At about nine, famished and exhausted as they all were, he stopped pumping, moved across deck and urged upon the captain a possible course of action.

The captain agreed. Newton turned his back towards the pumps. Spontaneously he said: 'If this will not do, the Lord have mercy on us!'

The captain was astonished to overhear such a sentiment on the lips of John Newton, this youth with scars of a naval flogging on his back, and of slave chains on his ankles, and a tongue so acid in its blasphemies that it shocked hardbitten mariners. The captain had taken him from a remote West African shore in obedience to strict instructions from England, having found him by an amazing coincidence and overborne his reluctance to come home. The captain had long wished he had never set eyes on the fellow – and now he was calling on the Lord!

Newton himself suddenly realized that he had uttered a prayer. At once he thought: 'What mercy can there be for me? What mercy for *me*? What –'

A log fell from the grate. The Reverend John Newton woke from his cat-nap with a start. The vivid dream about that dreadful day, long ago, lay strong in his newly-awake mind, with the memory of that unpremeditated prayer which he had spoken above the wind and the rush of water and the creaking of the pumps.

He could only wonder afresh at the amazing grace of God.

The way to a strong faith had been slow, hard, and was packed with adventures as the years before; but that moment on 10 March 1748 as he faced death by drowning in the North Atlantic had begun the process which had transformed him from a libertine and atheist.

Newton rose from his chair by the fire and sat at his desk. He had his hymn for the prayer meeting. Dipping his quill he wrote in his small, neat hand the first verse:

> *Amazing grace (how sweet the sound)*
> *That saved a wretch like me!*
> *I once was lost, but now am found,*
> *Was blind, but now I see.*

*   *   *

The exact circumstances of the writing of *Amazing Grace* have never been discovered; if Newton told anyone, the conversation was not noted down or the letter is lost. The only clue is the verse of Scripture with which he introduced it in *Olney Hymns*. Therefore the above account is no more than reasonable conjecture.

Of the facts behind the hymn there can be no doubt. What follows in this book may be extraordinary but it is true – the story of 'a wretch', a prodigal son, lost and 'blind', who was saved by amazing grace to become one of the best loved hymn writers of the Christian church, a preacher, evangelist and author who left his mark on his age, the one-time slaver who helped to destroy the Slave Trade.

Part One

A WRETCH LIKE ME

1

The Captain's Boy

The White Tower of the Tower of London shimmered in the sun. Tall masts and spars filled London Pool, little boats darted back and forth between the shipping. The whole scene was alive with the sights and sounds of England's commerce and pride.

Watching it from the quarter deck of a merchantman, one spring day of 1732, stood a small boy of six: John, only child of Captain John Newton, master of a vessel preparing for another Mediterranean voyage. Captain Newton liked to take his son on board whenever he checked the loading of cargo or the repairing of sails and tackle; then they would be rowed back to Wapping Stairs whence the captain, with self-conscious dignity, walked the few hundred yards home, with John following in tense silence a pace or two behind.

John lived almost in terror whenever his father returned from a voyage, for the Captain showed himself as strict a disciplinarian to his small family in their neat house in Wapping as he did to his crew. John must jump to orders like a cabin boy, stand until told to sit, keep silent unless addressed. Laughter in the presence of the Captain was insubordination unless the sea dog laughed first. He never displayed affection for his son although later on he would prove his love again and again when John's misdeeds might have forfeited it for ever.

The Captain was a curious mixture. Educated by Jesuits

17

in Spain, where his father had gone out as a merchant or a master mariner, he remained a Protestant of strict principles, if without open religious feelings, but his habits and gait carried a flavour of Don Quixote: he walked as if he were a hidalgo with a hundred quarterings and a vast estate, instead of a quarter-deck and a small house, where the neighbours, mostly sea officer families and small merchants, thought him rather ridiculous. Yet he was a sound seaman, highly regarded by shipowners and his fellow captains.

John's mother, Elizabeth Newton, came from a Dissenter family, and her character was such a contrast to her husband's that it must have been a surprising match. She mixed little with the neighbours, she was deeply religious, and she disliked the expeditions to the anchored shipping which took her boy away from her eye. She dreaded lest his sharp memory retain sailor oaths or bawdy sailor songs, or that he catch a glimpse of a half-dead pirate hanging in chains from the gallows on Wapping mudbank, where three full tides must wash over a corpse before burial. She was more relieved than sad when the Captain once again bade a formal farewell and strutted down the street to disappear for months on another voyage.

She could then indulge her greatest delight: educating John. She lay coughing on a couch, a Spanish shawl clutched about her and a book in her hand, hearing him recite improving rhymes and the answers to Isaac Watts' catechisms for the young. John learned the multiplication table and the rudiments of Latin, which she had taught herself first, and developed a neat handwriting by copying hers.

This life appealed to John more than running around with other boys. His mother remained the only friend he wanted. For much of a year the reminders of his father were their trinkets from Spain and Venice and the Levant, and a shadowy dread of his return, but she was his to enjoy: her brown hair tied neatly under her cap, the pallid face heightened by glistening red cheeks which were the sign of

18

the 'consumption' (tuberculosis) which was soon to carry her off. She had a merry laugh but jokes were private to themselves: the world knew her as grave, and quietly pious.

Every Sunday Mrs. Newton and John walked the short distance up the street to Prince's Square off the Radcliffe Highway, to the Dissenting chapel of Dr. David Jennings. His long prayers and sermons droned over the head of a small boy, yet the services left an indelible impression because Jennings had introduced the new hymns of Isaac Watts, whose own chapel stood a mile off within the City. The two pastors were friends and the puny head of the sickly, cheerful Watts sometimes peered over the Radcliffe Square pulpit. Whereas the parish church, where the Captain sometimes took John, sang nothing but metrical psalms, line by line after the parish clerk, the chapel sang Watts' hymns in chorus like sailors' shanties; a new concept in English hymn-singing and thrilling to a musical boy. One of Watts' hymns was famous already: *When I survey the wondrous cross.* They sang the second line as Watts originally wrote it: 'Where the young Prince of Glory died.' John sang with fervour in his high treble, right to the last line in which the young Prince of Glory 'shall have my life, my soul, my all.'

As mother and son walked home after chapel on Sunday mornings they could glimpse the shipping on the Thames. Those Sunday walks, up and back along the street, seemed to symbolize the two pulls on John's boyhood: to the pulpit, to the quarter-deck. His father planned that he should follow the family tradition and enter the Mediterranean trade, his mother that he go up to St. Andrews University in Scotland, with which David Jennings had links, and then enrol in his academy for preachers: the sea should not have her Jack.

The summer of 1732 put an end to such dreams. Elizabeth Newton's influence on her son had filtered deeper into his soul than he could realize. She had taught him that God had revealed His truth in the Bible, which must neither be doubted nor disobeyed, and that after death comes judgement. She had given him an ideal of purity and devotion which he might forget and betray but would never escape. Had she lived he might have learned her secret early in his career. Instead, though she was barely thirty years old, her cough grew worse, her face more pale and her eyes unnaturally bright.

A distant cousin and school friend, Elizabeth Churchill, who was married to a customs officer in Chatham called George Catlett, came on a visit and persuaded her to try the purer air of Kent. They boarded out John with a neighbour, under Dr. Jennings' kindly eye, and he last saw his mother enter a hackney carriage which took her and Mrs. Catlett across London Bridge, still with its houses, to their seats on the Chatham coach.

He expected her to return for his seventh birthday on 24 July 1732, but by then she was dead. They had left him behind to save him from watching her die. This was a disastrous decision. Had he gone to Chatham, and after his mother's death stayed with the Catletts for a while at least, he would have known 'Polly', their eldest child Mary, as a plump infant of three years old, becoming her adopted brother; instead, he first met her ten years later and fell hopelessly in love at an impossible time.

His life might have shaped differently, and dreams not turn to nightmares before they came true beyond all imagining.

*   *   *

Months, years could pass without news of a mariner. With his father possibly shipwrecked and drowned, or enslaved by Barbary pirates, John felt an orphan already, with no dear confidant, no pilot, no landmark at which to steer. He resolved to honour his mother's memory by growing up to be a preacher, but the young Prince of Glory seemed as remote as a planet in the sky; nor did the name

20

of Jesus sound sweet in John Newton's ear. Then the sea blood stirred in his veins and he vowed he would sail with his father. Drifting mentally this way and that he continued through autumn and winter until the cessation of Atlantic storms allowed the Mediterranean ships to bring back their cargoes of spices and silks.

Captain Newton walked up Wapping Stairs one day in the spring of 1733 and discovered the door of his home locked and hung with faded crêpe, and his black-suited son in a house nearby. The Captain showed no emotion nor allowed his son to weep. Instead he found him a step-mother by promptly marrying again.

His bride's surname is not known (nor is that of John's mother) but she bore the unusual Christian name of Thomasin and came from Essex. The Newtons loaded their household goods on a waggon and journeyed down the Tilbury road to the parish of Aveley. Here, on a farm looking down the marshes to the Thames and the low Kentish hills beyond, they made their home with Thomasin's father, a substantial tenant grazier, who could look after them when the Captain returned to the sea.

Until the age of eleven, John Newton now suffered the fate of the unloved stepson, compounded by miserably unhappy terms away at a private school on the Essex-Middlesex border. Its headmaster was a tyrant of the cane and birch-rod. He turned John from a child who had learned much at his mother's knee into a boy who knew little except how to take a beating, until, in John's second year, a new young usher noticed that he was not the idiot he seemed, and aroused his enthusiasm for Latin. He reached the top of the class, but the usher pushed too fast and John forgot most of his Latin as soon as he left the school. His memory of the school was horrible but probably it taught him more than he allowed, for he could write a good hand, read a well argued book and, as he grew older, master the mathematics required in a sea officer.

His father, when at home during John's holidays, kept him in fear and bondage, breaking his spirit. And stopped his formal education too soon: on his eleventh birthday, 24 July 1736, John Newton boarded his father's ship at Long Reach, where the Thames runs close to Aveley, and sailed for the Mediterranean on the first of five voyages which, in the next six years, gave him a solid grounding in seamanship but no love for his father. The Captain cushioned him from the crew yet imposed a sterner discipline on his son than on a cabin boy, hardening his body and roughening his character.

Back home in Essex – for the Captain did not take his son on every voyage but left him ashore for months at a time – the young Newton ran wild with the village lads, for he was full of fun when left to himself. His half-brother William, baptized at Aveley parish church on 8 September 1736, absorbed the affections of step-mother and of the old grazier, and neither of them cared what he did away from the farmhouse. Sailor oaths and stories picked up when out of his father's eye gave him leadership in all kinds of mischief such as poaching: the great house at Aveley, an exquisite red brick mansion called Belhus, stood empty and in bad repair because the young landowner, Thomas Barrett-Lennard, afterwards Lord Dacre, lived elsewhere with an aunt. The deer in his park were targets for risky adventures; detection would lead at the very least to a sound thrashing from a gamekeeper.

These years of puberty, when Newton was neither a country boy nor a seaman but a little of both, fell into a curious oscillating pattern. Two incidents stand out.

He had free use of his step-grandfather's horses when not required and he loved to whip up speed. One day as he cantered along a lane he noticed with the corner of his eye that the hedgerows had been layered, leaving large jagged spikes of brushwood to tear out an eye or pierce a brain. At that moment the horse stumbled and threw him and he

22

missed a spike by inches. Unhurt, he was shaken to realize that had he been thrown half a degree differently the spike would have impaled and, quite probably, projected him without warning Before Jehovah's Awful Throne, as Dr. Watts put it in The Old Hundredth. Memories flooded back: the hymn singing in chapel; the teaching of his mother, now canonized as a saint in Newton's mind; the devout intentions long since forgotten; the old certainties of heaven and hell and judgement.

He stopped swearing, kept away from rowdy youths, read religious books which he had found among his mother's belongings, and said his prayers. No one guided him between truth and error, and his new piety puffed his contempt for the earth-bound household at Aveley and the mumbling vicar. After two or three months, however, the old urges gradually pushed out the piety and he ran wild again.

The second incident had more lasting effect.

A man-of-war lay anchored in Long Reach. A waterman had promised Newton and other boys to row them out on the Sunday afternoon, for in addition to admiring the guns and holy-stoned decks, and the paintwork and rigging kept smarter than any merchantman's, a young sea dog of the merchant service could gloat over the wretched Jack Tars who lived under the rattan, the rope's end and the cat. Excited all morning, chaffing at the length of the sermon and then at the old grazier slowly eating his roast, Newton left the table at last to run and walk the two or three miles to Purfleet jetty. He arrived too late. He fumed to see the boatload of visitors, his best friend among them, nearing the man-of-war. Suddenly the boat hit an underwater hazard and turned turtle. His friend and several others drowned before his eyes.

At the funeral a chastened John Newton repented once again, this time upholding his religion for two full years of asceticism, whether on shore or at sea; yet he would still join escapades, easing his conscience by gabbling prayers in the belief that these would balance naughtiness when weighed Before Jehovah's Awful Throne.

Village lads and shipmates alike rated him peculiar, and when his father put him as a pupil with an English merchant at Alicante in Spain, and sailed away from the landlocked bay to the east, the man soon did not know what to make of a lad who daydreamed at his ledger desk and resented attempts to teach him trade; who had a merry smile and got into mischief, yet rose early to read devotional books. The merchant handed him back on the Captain's return voyage.

2

Polly

A landscape of brick houses stretched back from the quayside – the Dutch port of Middleburg, an unlikely place to alter the direction of John Newton's life.

He went ashore from his father's ship, a dreamy youth of nearly seventeen with no close friends or particular ambition except to avoid the displeasure of the captain who also was his parent. He wandered up a street where every shop had it sign which creaked above the heads of the passers by. He looked vaguely at the goods displayed, heard the apprentices shout their wares in a strange tongue, stepped into the gutter to avoid a fat burgher and, on impulse, entered a shop which sold odds and ends and books. His eye caught a title in English.

It was the second volume of the celebrated *Characteristics* by the philosopher Earl of Shaftesbury, written some thirty years before. The heading of one of the two treatises within intrigued John Newton: *The Moralists: A Philosophical Rhapsody*. He bought the book, began to read, and was at once absorbed in the argument.

They crossed the Channel after unloading their Levantine cargo and sailed up the Thames. They paid off and the Newtons rode into Essex. During long lazy hours at Aveley in the summer of 1742 John read and re-read *A Philosophical Rhapsody*, holding the book close to his face as he was short-sighted, until he almost knew by heart this charming conversation-piece. He thought it most religious because the characters spoke often of God, though never of Christ and His cross; this Lord Shaftesbury had been an early Deist, of the kind that became common in the half century following his death in 1713.

Shaftesbury's words insinuated into John Newton as he stood on the verge of manhood the idea that he must forget his dead mother's gentle insistence that goodness and wisdom grew best from obedience to God's truth revealed in the Bible. To Shaftesbury, as Newton understood him at the time, Truth was no more than an opinion and every man must form his own. If he wished to become a truly moral man he must put away childish dependence on sacred writ and cultivate virtue by following the dictates of heart and mind wherever they led.

All this put Dr. Watts' hymns out of tune, for if Shaftesbury were right, the Young Prince of Glory could be no more than a long dead moralist, a philosopher of a distant age. Years later, when John Newton, in more senses than one, had come home after his incredible adventures, he said that Shaftesbury's book had operated like a slow poison and had prepared the way for all that followed.

Certainly if Newton had not taken Shaftesbury's advice that summer, to follow the dictates of his own heart wherever they should lead, he would not have become embroiled in a chain of events the following winter, which, starting on 12 December 1742, set in motion one of the eighteenth century's most extraordinary sagas.

It began with a coincidence, the first of many which mark Newton's story.

His father, after the voyage which touched Middleburg, had retired from the sea, taken a responsible shore post with the Royal Africa Company and bought a house in London. He placed John as third mate under another Mediterranean captain, who reported on their return that this dreamy lad would never make a sailor worthy of the Newton name. Thereupon Captain Newton wrote to a Liverpool shipowner,

26

a close friend named Joseph Manesty who had interests in slaves and sugar in Jamaica. On opening the reply the Captain summoned his son to hear good news: Manesty promised to make John's fortune; he should go to a Jamaican plantation as an overseer of slaves, with the prospect of being a planter before he was thirty. If he showed himself shrewd, hard and laborious he might return one day from the island to buy a fine estate and enter Parliament.

John liked the prospect. He would be waited on by slaves and wield power while retaining his dream world: Shaftesbury's characters in *A Rhapsody* might have been planters, for they never soiled their hands with manual labour. Newton gladly bought all he needed for a voyage to the tropics.

A few days before he was due to board the coach to Liverpool to take ship for Jamaica a letter, a rare event in itself, reached him in London. He did not recognize the hand but on breaking the seal he recognized the name from a long distant past: Elizabeth Catlett, his mother's dearest friend in whose house she had died. Mrs. Catlett had not approved Captain Newton's hasty remarriage and the two families had severed relations, but no doubt she had promised her dying friend to remember her son, since the two of them had lightly plotted that Elizabeth Newton's John should grow up to marry Elizabeth Catlett's Mary ('Polly') who was now nearly fourteen. Mrs. Catlett's letter enquired after John's welfare and invited him to stay should ever he be near Chatham.

She had waited ten years to write. With no knowledge of his plans she had chosen the moment when he was to disappear for prolonged absence overseas. Even more of a coincidence, her invitation reached him when he was about to ride into her part of Kent, for his father had ordered him to do some small business near Maidstone. The Catletts lived half a mile off his road.

The Captain granted him leave to call on the Catletts.

Yet when John reached the turn on his homeward journey on 12 December 1742 he felt indifferent, and only the prospect of a hot meal by the fire determined him to dismount at their door. He blew on his fingers and wrapped his cloak tighter in the bitter cold as he waited an answer to his knock, and looked around at a solid, not stately home, suitable to a customs officer's station in life, and the neat frostbound garden.

The door was opened, not by a serving maid but by a girl of the house, whom he knew must be Polly. Her mother, coming up behind, ran forward before he could announce himself and kissed her old friend's features which she saw in his face. She pulled him inside, gave orders for his horse to be stabled and fed, and at once made John feel at home. She told him to call her and Catlett 'uncle' and 'aunt' and to stay as long as he liked.

The family crowded round and he felt he had known them all his life. The younger daughter Elizabeth and eleven year old John treated him as a big brother who had seen the world; Sarah, aged four, and Susanna, aged two, looked on with wide eyes; George was a baby in his cradle.

Newton quickly became aware, in a very special way, of Polly. She seemed different from any girl he had met. Bashful, well grown, with a dimple and a smile, her kindness and simplicity drew him until only good breeding stopped him calling her, then and there, 'My dearest sweetest dear Polly.' She was not a great beauty. She was less intelligent than he, wrote an awkward rounded hand and could not spell. She sang sweetly and had an ear for verses; her mother and the nearby school for young ladies had taught her deportment, dancing and the household arts, and she could command the obedience and affection of the younger Catletts. Innocence and purity were self-evident, but she enjoyed a frolic and laughter. None of this explains why Newton, at seventeen, should have fallen head over heels in love within a few hours of setting eyes on Polly Catlett.

28

He had never been in love and did not know what afflicted him, why he was restless in her absence, tongue-tied and confused in her company. That night he hardly slept for thinking of her. Next morning he scarcely dared a glance.

Polly was unaware that she had captured this gawky sailor, that he was her prize, ready to haul down his colours and lay them at her feet as the fair captain of his destiny. Newton could not declare his love, being almost penniless and a mere youth, yet he longed to know whether she returned it. He swore to himself he would make a fortune to throw at her feet, yet he could not bear to leave her for the other side of the globe. Three days passed like a dream. A fourth went by and still Newton stayed, and the Catletts, unaware that he was bound for Jamaica, did not hurry him to saddle his horse. Love-crazed, he lingered until the West India ship must have sailed: his heart had dictated that the Atlantic should not sever him from Polly.

Thus Christmas passed at Chatham gaily; in London, his father and John's stepmother were miserable with anxiety lest he had been murdered by a highwayman or, more likely, taken by the Navy's press gang, the terror of every merchant sailor ashore. The days ticked by in silence, for John did not dare write the real reason for his absence and could not bear to concoct a false one.

He rode home after three weeks. The Captain received him in anger, but forgave quickly, having secretly regretted that his son would have left the sea. For punishment, he must sail a voyage as a common sailor. John thought it a small price for the hope of seeing Polly again within the year.

This voyage to the Levant did much to drive away his dreamy idleness. He learned to step lively to avoid punishment, to haul on the capstan singing the shanties, to eat hardtack instead of the captain's bread. He smoked a clay pipe, swore with the best, swapped bawdy stories. In the tumble of the fo'c'sle he lost his resolve to pursue virtue in the manner of Shaftesbury; even the shadowy Deity who had displaced the crucified Prince of Glory seemed more a figment of imagination. Serving before the mast stripped from John Newton most of his innocence.

He still remained a virgin. At the age of eighteen he rated fornication the ultimate profligacy, so he did not follow his friends into brothels.

And Polly held his heart. He dared to claim in middle age that none of the scenes of misery and wickedness he afterwards knew had banished her for a single hour from his thoughts. 'How wonderful,' he mused, 'that when we were both so young, an impression should be made on my mind, almost at first sight, which neither distance nor absence, nor all my sufferings, nor even all the licentiousness and folly I afterwards ran into, could obliterate!'

3

The Lost Ring

The glories of Venice, where the ship had spent several days taking in cargo, had slipped below the horizon before dusk. Young Newton, who now was homeward bound, swung his hammock and fell asleep with delicious thoughts of Polly.

He dreamed not of Polly but of Venice. He was back in the harbour at night, on watch, pacing the deck alone. A stranger appeared, in his hand a ring which glinted in the moonlight, suggesting a valuable stone. He gave the ring to Newton.

'Preserve it carefully,' said the stranger. 'While you do so, you will be happy and successful. If you lose it or part with it, you must expect nothing but trouble and misery.'

Newton slipped the ring on to his finger with expressions of gratitude. The stranger disappeared as suddenly as he had come and Newton resumed his pacing, not in the least doubting that he could preserve the ring, and glad to have future happiness in his own keeping.

A second stranger materialized. He commented on the ring, but when Newton told him its secret power, the man laughed, ridiculing such a simple belief. 'The thing is impossible,' he said, and went on to prove it by logic. 'Throw the ring away!' he urged.

Shocked, Newton argued back, until the other's blend of mockery and reasoning induced doubt. Doubt grew into certainty, mixed with shame that he had believed the first stranger's promise, until Newton impulsively pulled the ring from his finger. He dropped it over the side.

Fire burst from the distant mountains — vivid, horrifying, a judgement on his folly. The tempter, in tones of disgust, then said: 'All the mercy God had in store for you was comprised in that ring which you have wilfully thrown away. Now you must go to the burning mountain. These flames have been kindled for you!'

John Newton stood tongue-tied with terror, waiting without plea or hope to be marched to his fate. But a third person (or it might have been the ring's donor) approached him and asked why he shook in fear. Newton confessed and the dream-figure reprimanded him, then asked: 'Do you think you will be wiser if you have the ring again?'

Before Newton could answer the man jumped into the water and recovered it. As he climbed on board again the flames in the mountains went out, the tempter fled, and in joy and thanks Newton stretched out his hand for the ring.

The man withheld it. He said: 'If you were entrusted with this ring again you would very soon bring yourself into the same distress. You are unable to keep it! But I will preserve it for you. And whenever it is needed I will produce it on your behalf.'

This strange dream haunted Newton as they sailed the Adriatic and westward towards Spain, and prodded him to resume 'the orderly pursuit of virtue' for many weeks; yet before he stepped ashore at Wapping Stairs in December 1743 he had forgotten his good intentions.

Captain Newton welcomed John home. Satisfied that sentence had been served and disobedience purged, he at once procured him an officer's berth; if he did well he might be master of his own ship within a few years. John would sail very soon; Christmas leave would be brief, but his father gave him permission to visit the Catletts. He warned him, however, to be on guard against a press gang, for the rumour ran that France was about to attack England in the dispute over the Austrian Succession. The veteran reminded the boy that His Majesty's ships would be looking for merchant seamen to press into a Royal Navy expanding to a war footing: he must keep the sharpest watch, for until he joined the merchantman he could not carry the certificate of protection which compelled a press gang to leave a serving seaman alone.

The Catletts turned January into summer by their warmth of hospitality. Polly smiled at him. Newton did not declare his love, for if he now had prospects he lacked means, and no youth of eighteen in the reign of George II would presume to approach the parent of a girl even younger for permission to ask her hand. The unsuspecting Catletts treated the two as brother and sister.

Days passed too swiftly. Newton could not bear to leave Polly, a magnet stronger than the berth his father had secured. Once again, irresponsible and ungrateful, the boy wrecked his father's plans. He overstayed his leave, missed his ship and returned to an irate parent.

Newton's life story hinged on that disobedience, for had he joined his ship he would have been safe, sailing the seas, on the fatal First of March, 1744, the day on which calamity fell.

His father had nearly thrown him over but relented and again used his influence on John's behalf. Before the Captain had found him a ship the Newtons went down to the Essex farm and this proved John's undoing. Aveley being near the ferry to the Dover Road which passes Chatham, he could not resist the opportunity of riding to Polly. He forgot his father's warning that the River at the outbreak of war was dangerous to a seaman; he forgot to make enquiry before crossing to the Kentish shore, though news always spread of a naval press. He walked straight into a press gang.

They knew he was a sailor by his gait. Implacable, ignoring his plea that he had served as an officer and should not be taken into the Navy as a common seaman, they thrust him under guard into the backroom of an inn while the press looked for further prey. He was allowed to scribble a note and pay a lad to take it across the river to Aveley. If, twice before in Kent, John Newton had hidden his whereabouts, he turned desperately now to his father, whose not inconsiderable influence might save him. Hours passed; nine other wretches were thrust into the little room; at last John heard his father's voice outside, and listened to him speak urgently as one sea officer to another, and heard the young lieutenant of the press reply respectfully.

There was no hint of concession in the lieutenant's tone, and Captain Newton came sadly into the backroom to tell John that lack of a 'protection' had proved fatal. The French were already at sea and shots had been exchanged although war had not been declared (the recent southwest gale had in fact dispersed a French fleet off Dunkirk and stopped an attempt to land a Jacobite force in Kent, headed by the Young Pretender). The lieutenant would not release a well-built lad who had been excellently trained at sea by his own father.

The horrors that John knew by hearsay must be tasted to the full. He and the other nine were marched to the quay, brought downriver in the *Betsey* tender to the Nore and put on board H.M.S. *Harwich*, a fourth rate (fifty guns) man-of-war, on Sunday 4 March. Rough hands hustled them below to a dark hole below the waterline which offered no opportunity to dive overboard before they were legally impressed, when disappearance would become desertion. In the tender and now in the ship, Newton suffered something of the airless confinement he would afterwards inflict upon African slaves. Then he was ordered to strip. Mr. Bacon the surgeon passed him fit. Soon the recruits were marched at a run to the Captain.

Philip Carteret, captain of H.M.S. *Harwich*, was related to Lord Carteret, one of the King's principal Secretaries of State, and came from a distinguished naval family. Newton was fortunate in that Carteret was a good seaman and humane. He examined each recruit about their sea experience and ordered 'John Newtown' (as the clerk entered him on the muster roll) to be impressed at the higher rate of Able Seaman, together with John Craven and James Wheeler. The other six were impressed as Ordinary Seamen.

H.M.S. *Harwich* set sail for convoy duty on 8 March, taking advantage of the freshening wind which destroyed the Jacobite's last hope of crossing the Narrows that spring. For John Newton, the voyage was a misery of pain, fatigue, fear and hunger. Spurred by the rattan cane swung expertly by the master at arms, Mr. Hedge, or the rope's end 'starter' in the hands of George Murris the bosun, or his mates, Newton and the other new men made every movement on deck at the double, and up the rigging in quick time. Driven until they would have dropped were it not for fear of worse pain, fed shamefully, although Jos Vincent, quartermaster, may have been less corrupt and inefficient than many, they were virtually slaves. The eighteenth century believed that a man-of-war's seaman would never endure the physical and mental strain of working the ship in all weathers and fighting the enemy unless first broken, and kept thereafter in dread of corporal punishment: his early training was the naval equivalent of a black slave's 'seasoning' on arrival in the West Indies.

The misery was compounded by the company which Newton had joined, three hundred men in the confined space of one of the Royal Navy's smaller fighting ships; H.M.S. *Harwich*, built two years earlier, was a hundred and forty feet long and forty feet wide. Few if any of the lower deck were volunteers. At every gaol delivery the judge would sentence a quota of convicted criminals to naval service; other youths had been handed to naval press by offended parents or outraged masters, others had ruined themselves and could see no future except enlistment; the rest had been seized by the press. Newton, familiar enough with rough ways and speech in a merchantman's crew was disgusted by naval profaneness and debauchery. The lower deck provoked in him a sense of superiority. He lessened his own profanity and attempted to live cleanly, if only to display that he was neither jailbird nor lout but a sea captain's son. And always he kept alive a slender hope: that the sea captain parent might achieve his rescue. Otherwise, nothing lay ahead beyond his nineteenth birthday except hardship.

On 3 April, after one month on the lower deck, Newton paraded with all hands to hear Captain Carteret read the Declaration of War with France. A day or two later Newton was ordered before him, and no able seaman received such a summons without fear. The Captain, however, spoke kindly. He said that a man he would gladly serve had asked him to favour the son of Captain John Newton of the Royal Africa Company and therefore he proposed to take him on the quarter-deck as a Midshipman. His father did not wish him discharged from the Royal Navy in wartime, when honour and prize money might come his way.

From being almost a slave Newton entered the comparative comfort of the gunroom, and from jumping to the command of men he despised he could lord it over former messmates. This sudden change of fortune brought out the worst in him. Midshipman Newton delighted in displaying power over Cullpack, Tarrant and the others who had shared his misery on the tender. He resented the discipline of the quarter-deck, and though skilful professionally he was sullen, and worked no harder than if he still served in the Mediterranean trade. He did not repay the kindness of Captain Carteret; which was not only ungrateful but foolish, for a man-of-war's captain is an absolute monarch. Thus he prepared for himself a fearful future which he might have foreseen had he not forgotten, in folly and pride, that power derives from duty.

Throughout May 1744 *Harwich* escorted convoys to Scotland and Norway, a dreary task leaving hours of boredom.

These the gunroom dispersed by animated discussions led by the captain's clerk, James Mitchell, a man in his twenty-third or fourth year who became Newton's particular mentor and friend. Observant, well read, with an engaging manner and a touch of amusement in his voice as he demolished arguments or exposed ignorance, Mitchell noticed that Newton still had some religious views and a conscience, and at first he avoided ridicule of either. Instead, having gained Newton's confidence he disputed his interpretation of *Characteristics*, and argued that Shaftesbury sought to supplant, not support religion. A mature man, said Mitchell, had no need of devotion to a God who, if He existed, was nothing but an impersonal First Cause. Obeying such a deity did not make for happiness or success; parting with Him did not bring trouble. Newton was shocked. But like the tempter in the dream near Venice, the argument sowed doubt. Mitchell then broke his colours at the masthead, as it were, and disclosed himself as a freethinker.

He insinuated his sentiments in the most plausible way. Religion, Mitchell would suggest as they leaned over the poop idly watching the vessel's wake, is the harness by which proud teachers impose their opinions with threats of judgement or hopes of immortality. The wise man subscribes to no opinions but his own, formed by experience as broad as he can gain. Death is extinction; conscience, Mitchell would add, is merely the doubting of the immature: the grown man does as he pleases, giving the desires of body or mind free play, thus fulfilling himself in the only life he will have. If a desire exists it should be expressed: Mitchell claimed that Lord Shaftesbury's view had its echo in the well-known line from Alexander Pope, who died at Twickenham that very May: 'Whatever is, is right.'

Newton's ideas lacked substance enough to withstand such good humoured logic which, moreover, pointed him to a path he had itched to travel. His self-will and growing sensuality had long chafed at the restraints of his mother's

Christian faith and morals as they lingered in his conscience. If Mitchell's teaching were right, Newton would be released, body and soul, free to indulge sexual appetites because fornication would no longer be sin to him, and free to believe any creed or none. The prospect grew daily more attractive.

Mitchell pressed his advantage. At length there came a day, somewhere off the coast of Norway that early summer of 1744, when John Newton plucked the ring of conscience and Christian faith from his finger and dropped it over the side.

No mountains burst into flame.

4

Naval Deserter

Midshipman Job Lewis was a steady youth who held to the principles he had learned in a good home. He looked up to Newton, older, and with years of sea experience; enjoyed his songs on deck, and smoked many a pipe with him in the gunroom. Lewis had noted with approval on Newton's first arrival on the quarter deck that he had a little religion and lived cleanly when they put into port.

Now Newton began to ridicule Job Lewis's religious feelings and to glory in atheism as the only creed for a man. He set out to make Job an infidel and a libertine.

They were still arguing when H.M.S. *Harwich* went into action in the North Sea, the only naval skirmish in which John Newton served. It began in the early afternoon of 30 September off the Yorkshire coast when the lookout at the masthead saw three sail to the northwest. Carteret gave chase, clearing the ship for action and ordering the men to stand to their guns. After two hours under full sail they closed on a single man-of-war which broke the French colours. At 6 p.m. *Harwich* opened fire with one of her fo'c'sle guns and kept it up as the distance narrowed, also firing a twelve-pounder out of the head door, while the enemy kept firing her stern gun without inflicting damage.

At half past six *Harwich* closed with her prey – the privateer *Solide* of Dunkirk – and gave her a destructive broadside from the upper deck and seven of the lower deck guns, while the Frenchman's broadside and hand grenades slightly damaged the rigging and wounded one man. As *Solide* fell astern, Carteret wore ship and prepared to give her another broadside when, to the cheers of the British, she struck her colours as daylight faded. Carteret sent boarders. The boats brought back her captain – one Sourbert – and Newton and his brother midshipmen and officers watched on the quarter-deck as the Frenchman surrendered his sword.

Encouraged by the prize money they would all receive they continued the dull routine of patrol and convoy, and Newton resumed his assault on the faith of Job Lewis. He succeeded, destroying it more completely than he realized until they met again nine years later, in poignant circumstances.

Yet inwardly, at first, Newton did not believe his own atheism. While accusing Job of hypocrisy he had been a hypocrite himself, hiding a gnawing anguish of conscience under big words and forced smiles. On night watch he disliked being alone with his thoughts. When off watch he would wake suddenly in the small hours, tortured by remorse, worried for the future, arguing mentally with persistent thoughts of the God he denied. The young Prince of Glory would not leave him alone.

Newton hardened himself. He had taken the freethinker's road and would not turn back. Intimations of immortality grew fainter until 'I believed my own lie.' He would say sadly in after years: 'Like an unwary sailor who quits his port just before a rising storm, I renounced the hopes and comforts of the gospel at the very time when every other comfort was about to fail me.'

This 'rising storm', this loss of all comfort, he brought on his own head. The innocent cause was Polly Catlett.

During the summer his ship had moored for several weeks in the mouth of the Medway at Sheerness, whence Newton often took boat for Chatham. Polly now boarded at a seminary for young ladies, where he pursued her in his fine uniform, daydreaming of his exquisite powers of gallantry. These never materialized in her presence: indeed her companions laughed at him as nautical and lubberly and teased Polly until she begged that if he must, he should only visit her when she went home. She knew he loved her and she instinctively, artlessly kept her guard, neither encouraging too positively nor implying an absolute refusal. He took care never to wear his new colours as a freethinker and atheist when he sailed in Polly's waters. More than once he overstayed his leave, to the annoyance of Captain Carteret; prudence went overboard with Polly in the offing.

Soon after the action against the privateer Newton learned that *Harwich* might leave home waters for a year in the Mediterranean. On his next visit to Chatham he promised Polly to return with prize money and promotion. He dared not ask her hand formally, for fear of rebuff, but implored her to remember him when she came out into Chatham society and men better skilled in the arts and niceties of the polite world proposed to her. She must suspend her answer for a year for the sake of the absent suitor whose affection, and desire to make her happy, far exceeded that of any other.

At Christmas time 1744 *Harwich* lay in the Downs, the great sea anchorage off Deal, north of the straits of Dover. To Newton's dismay and distress he discovered that the squadron's destination had been changed. As soon as the wind veered into a favourable quarter they would sail, not for the Mediterranean but the Cape of Good Hope and the far East Indies: instead of one year he would be away five. If he survived to return at all he would be twenty-four and Polly nineteen and almost certainly in another man's arms.

He must see her once more. He asked Captain Carteret for leave. The ship rode at single anchor, ready to sail at short notice, and Carteret, though disposed to be friendly despite Newton's disobedience, could grant only twenty-four hours. Yet Chatham lay a hard day's ride from Deal.

Even if Newton spent a bare hour with Polly and rode back through the night, and if the winter roads were not too muddy, and his hired hack showed the spirit of a thorough-bred, he could not be back on board in time.

His motto at this time was 'Never Deliberate'. On landing from the liberty boat he went to the livery stables and took horse for the Canterbury road, following the dictates of his passion.

At Chatham, instead of blowing hasty kisses and remount-ing after a hasty meal he stayed several days. Though he was still filled with silly confusion in Polly's presence, their gloom at the prospect of five years' absence betrayed the seriousness of their feelings, which previously her parents had dismissed as children's affection.

The Catletts knew by now that the lad had twice thrown away his future for Polly. This tokened a disastrous match. 'Uncle' Catlett ordered him out of the house: he must never see Polly again until Catlett gave him formal permission. The 'Aunt', Mrs. Catlett, showed more tenderness. She spoke to John as if to her own child, and promised that she would not object to an engagement in a better future; until then he must not call if Polly were at home, unless either he abandoned his suit or brought his father's written permission to continue it. She also forbade him to write, but Polly and he managed to make a secret arrangement for letters, possibly through a friendly maiden aunt who lived nearby.

Throughout the visit Newton had suffered dread of Captain Carteret, and this intensified as he cantered into Deal on the evening of 1 January 1745. He managed to see George Derby, the First Lieutenant, and to soften his heart by the true tale of love so that Derby prevailed on an angry Captain not to punish too harshly. However, Newton lost Carteret's favour, never to regain it. The storm gathered nearer.

The squadron lay in the Downs all January. Newton on night watches solaced his loneliness by holding imaginary conversations with Polly, and later one night wrote her a long letter which reached her by their secret route. She kept it all her life and it survives, the earliest Newton manuscript, signed with his monogram of J superimposed on N. He wrote gloomily of disappointments, his fear of losing her to a local swain, his belief that the voyage ahead would ruin or make him. He hoped for prize money, not merely on his own account, 'for I shall not value riches but for the opportunity of laying them at your feet.'

At last, a brave show of canvas and pennants to landsmen watching from the white cliffs of Dover or Beachy Head, the squadron sailed down Channel. Throughout February, at anchor in Spithead, Newton's fear of losing Polly while he sweated and fought in some distant clime preyed on his mind. On 23 February *Harwich* sailed with a fleet under Commodore George Pocock, flying his flag in H.M.S. *Sutherland*, and a convoy of Indiamen and Guinea ships. After three days the wind veered south westerly and forced fleet and convoy into Torbay. Then it changed again almost immediately and the Commodore led them out again, with disastrous consequences; several merchantmen and men-of-war went aground on Start Point.

Pocock ignored his losses and kept course westward until at nightfall on 28 February the fleet rounded the Lizard and met a violent gale blowing towards the Cornish coast. The fearful confusion of that roaring, moonless night, with too many vessels trying to avoid each other and a rocky lee shore, kept the whole ship's company working as Carteret's superb seamanship saved *Harwich* in several close calls. Morning revealed battered vessels on all quarters and the Commodore himself in a sorry plight with his mainmast and bowsprit gone. He ordered the fleet into Plymouth Sound.

March 1745 passed in repairing damage. The unexpected delay unsettled the crew. Stephen Forty and William Ramsey deserted, then Edward Armstrong and a trickle of other seamen, to Captain Carteret's annoyance. As for Newton, to be still in the same country as Polly Catlett quite maddened him, especially when he looked at the Guinea ships and knew that their men would be home within a year. Towards the end of the month he learned that his father was nearby at Dartmouth to inspect the damage sustained by the Africa Company. Surely, thought Newton, his father would find a way of exchanging his son out of the Navy into the Guinea service if only he could implore him face to face. But Carteret refused leave to go to Dartmouth: a midshipman who had abused his kindness could expect no favours.

On one of the first days of April the Captain ordered him to take a longboat party to fetch vegetables, fresh water and other supplies waiting on Plymouth quay. Since eleven men had run already and these shore trips gave the best opportunity, Carteret sharply reminded Newton to take utmost care that none of the people deserted.

As the longboat crew rowed him ashore, Newton suddenly decided to throw caution and duty to the winds, true to his maxim Never Deliberate. When they had made fast and the men's attention was absorbed in loading the casks he slipped aside and walked out of the Royal Navy for ever – or so he thought.

He adopted a deliberately jaunty air as he climbed westward from the town, checking his road to Dartmouth once he was far enough from the shipping. He walked on through the glory which is early spring in South Devon, and slept rough that night, not at an inn, for fear of meeting a suspicious naval person.

Next day he had passed through Morleigh and beneath the Roman encampments near Halwell and could see the high road from Totnes winding down towards the signpost where he must be less than two hours' walk from Dartmouth, his father, and freedom. Then, too late, he noticed a party of marines searching for deserters from ships wrecked in the storm. He could not avoid them. Nor, footsore, travelstained, lacking horse or carriage or written orders from his captain could he bluff them that he was either on duty or on leave. They arrested him, and marched him back the twenty-five weary miles to Plymouth, one of a motley set of absconded rascals taken on the run.

Shame at the stares of Plymouth citizens, who saw him hustled like a felon, gave way to indignation when he was kept two days in the guard house on shore. These emotions were nothing to the cold fear which crept upon him. Death was the penalty for desertion. If the Captain sent him to court-martial, Newton might be hanged from the yard arm, or awarded perhaps up to a hundred lashes with the cat o' nine tails: punishments were not as heavy as in the later part of the century. If Carteret dealt with the case summarily as absence without leave, not as desertion, a midshipman did not usually suffer more than a caning.

Newton at last found himself back on board, confined below in irons which manacled wrists and ankles. He lay raging at fate, dreading punishment, whilst unknown to him his father interceded through Admiral Medley for an exchange to a merchantman. Not surprisingly, Captain Carteret refused to grant what Newton had deserted to obtain. The boy had betrayed his trust and the Captain was implacable in resentment; but the humane Carteret did not have him court-martialled.

Newton in his autobiography passes over in six words what happened: 'I was publicly stripped and whipped.' All hands paraded on deck to witness punishment. As Carteret did not enter it in his log, and his punishment book does not survive, no evidence remains as to the severity, although by regulation no captain might award summarily more than a dozen lashes. This limit was seldom observed. Yet Carteret's character and Newton's youth alike point to the probability that two dozen would have been the very most. Twenty-four hard strokes on his bare back with a nine-tailed whip of knotted ropes, inflicted rather slowly with a roll of the drum between each, must have been exceedingly painful, though not crippling. For Newton, however, the physical agony was little to the searing disgrace as men he had bossed and abused could gloat to see him stripped and bloody. The proud freethinking disputant of the gunroom hung tied up like an animal. And it was a bosun's mate whom he had despised, on being promoted over his head, who now wielded the cat with all his strength.

The second part of Newton's punishment began when he was cut down from the gratings, sent below to the surgeon and ordered back to duty at the earliest moment that two hundred weals allowed. He returned, not as a midshipman but at the lowest rank of ordinary seaman; as he put it, 'brought down to the level of the lowest and exposed to the insults of all.' Those to whom he had been haughty and vain were not slow to get their own back, while former messmates of the gunroom who had watched his flogging with embarrassment and pity tried at first to shield him a little. They cooled quickly, not so much because of strict orders against softening the disgrace —ways could have been found without too much risk — but because Newton snarled like a wounded cur at the slightest touch of friendship.

Six years later Newton wrote that he had been 'degraded and punished as I well deserved'. When, however, he sailed from Plymouth for the Indies on 9 April 1745 he was filled with rage and injured pride, and with a sense that he had been grossly ill-used. The Captain took opportunities to display his continued resentment. Newton furiously meditated revenge, even to the limit of murder. 'My breast was filled with the most excruciating passions, eager desire, bitter rage and black despair. Every hour exposed me to some new insult or hardship, with no hope of relief or mitigation, no friend to take my part or to listen to my complaint.'

Worst of all, to his inflamed mind, was the loss of Polly.

He felt he had been torn from her forcibly. He would be absent five years and unlikely to see her again; if he did, it was improbable that he would return in a condition to claim her hand.

As *Harwich* sailed past the Lizard peninsula which gave a last sight of England for the westbound fleet, Newton, off-watch, placed himself by the gunwale. With inexpressible wistfulness and regret he gazed on the English shore. His thoughts were dismal; life offered nothing but darkness and misery. Death, to his atheist mind, would at least be extinction.

He kept his eyes on the receding coastline. When he could see it no longer, he would have flung himself into the sea. 'But the secret hand of God restrained me.'

5

The Slave Coast

The May sun beat down on the varied shipping in
Funchal roads, the chief anchorage of Madeira. In shallow
water H.M.S. *Harwich* lay heeled half over while the crew
greased the starboard side with tallow. Next day she was
heeled again to grease the larboard side. Ordinary Seaman
Newton might tire at this fatigue in the heat but he dared
now show it: the bosun and his mates made sure that his
sore back felt the touch of a 'starter' if he slacked. Even
worse was the labour of blacking the bends and painting the
sides with tar.

No misery, thought Newton as he splashed the hot tar,
could have been greater than his during the eighteen-day
passage from Plymouth. The quarter-deck mistrusted him,
the fo'c'sle despised him. Hated for the arrogance he had
displayed as a midshipman, he was driven exceptionally
hard by the petty officers. He had again contemplated
suicide. He wanted to murder Carteret too if a way offered
to effect murder and suicide together. One ray of hope made
him pause: that though the voyage would last five years, he
might see Polly again. Newton's love for her was the single
restraint left; he feared not God nor regarded man, yet he
could not bear that *she* should think meanly of him when he
was dead.

The labour seemed unending. Time was short because
the fleet was under orders to sail for the Cape on 10 May.
The fatigue of taking on fresh water in heavy casks, and all

manner of stores, consumed the hours of daylight and heat until the sailors wished they were dead. That night Newton slung his hammock and fell asleep in an instant and at first light next morning, Thursday 9 May 1745, he slept right through the bosun's whistle and the bustle as the rest of the watch stowed hammocks. One of the midshipmen made his rounds. He shook Newton awake, mingling jest with his order since they had been special friends in happier days in the gun-room. But when Newton insolently took time he drew out his dirk and cut down the hammock; that back still tender from the lashes hit the floor. Newton did not dare show his anger. Furious, he dressed, stowed hammock and went on deck.

The roads, with their backcloth of the mountain, looked busy enough. Among the men of war preparing for sea rode a few ships of the Guinea trade. Small boats plied between, or back and forth to the jetties. Then Newton saw a boat bobbing at *Harwich*'s ladder; one of his messmates, preparing to embark, had already dropped down his bundle. Newton asked where he was bound. The man replied that the Captain had pressed two skilled hands from the Guinea ship lying nearest, and the Commodore had ordered *Harwich* to supply two in their places: presumably the merchant captain, who had no legal right to refuse the naval press, had complained he would be undermanned.

Newton's heart instantly burned like fire. Here was his one hope. He begged that the boat be detained a few minutes and ran to the lieutenants and intreated them to intercede with the Captain that he be the other seaman dismissed from the ship. His motto, 'Never Deliberate,' had not changed, for reflection might have cautioned him not to expect good will from either lieutenants, since he had frequently angered both. However they had secretly pitied his flogging and expulsion from the quarter-deck and went to Captain Carteret. Carteret, perhaps glad to be rid of a bad lot, at once agreed to the exchange.

In little more than half an hour from being asleep John Newton was out of the Royal Navy. His determination at Plymouth, 'I will *not* go to India; I *will* go to Guinea,' was fulfilled. Had the midshipman made his rounds a few minutes later, had the Guinea ship's pressed men come aboard a few minutes earlier, the opportunity would have missed him. It was the second of the extraordinary coincidences – or providences as he would later term them – which shaped Newton's life.

It freed him from disgrace and the bondage of naval discipline. It lost him the officer who had made him an atheist and also, as he supposed, the midshipman whose religious faith Newton in his turn had destroyed. This man, Job Lewis, would reappear in his life but he never saw the ship again: H.M.S. *Harwich* served another fifteen years until wrecked off Cuba in 1760. Captain Carteret died in 1748.

Newton's brief crossing from man-of-war to Guinea ship was his Rubicon. He had joined H.M.S. *Harwich* a rather steady and studious youth, and pride had kept him above the habits of the herd. Neither conversion to atheism nor the degradation from the quarter-deck had snapped his resolution and when the whores of Funchal swarmed aboard he kept in check the animal passions which were all the stronger since the infliction of the corporal punishment. But now he would be among strangers who never knew the chaste youth he had once been. He need disguise no longer the man he had become. Years later he could distinctly recall, 'that while I was passing from the one ship to the other, this was one reason why I rejoiced in the exchange, viz., "that I now might be as abandoned as I pleased, without any control".' He was a few weeks short of his twentieth birthday.

The captain of the Guinea ship on questioning Newton exclaimed that he knew his father. He offered friendship and protection. The future looked assured, for this ship was engaged in the triangular Slave Trade which carried Sheffield goods, cloth, fire-arms and trinkets down the Windward coast of Africa to barter for slaves; shipped the slaves by the Middle Passage to the West Indies; then ran for home before the trade winds with a cargo of sugar and rum. Any captain or mate who survived the fevers long enough could rely on a good livelihood, while a landsman who superintended a 'factory' could make his fortune, like their passenger, Mr. Clow, the ship's part-owner who was returning from England. He had first landed on the coast as poor as Newton.

Thus Newton became a slaver. For the next six months of 1745 he sailed from river mouth to river mouth, down the coast and back, while Clow and the captain bargained with chiefs and factors for the slaves they had collected in their warehouses.

The crew always received slaves on board as enemies who would attempt to regain liberty. The blacks, after being duly bought, were branded and, as soon as ten or fifteen had been shipped, were put in irons. During the coastwise voyage the number of slaves increased, and the captain lost seamen by death or sickness, while others were absent in boats; thus he might have only ten men to watch over two hundred slaves and to work the ship. Therefore the crew confined the slaves below at night. In daytime, in fine weather, they brought them up by pairs, put a chain through a ring on their irons and locked this to ringbolts fastened at intervals on the deck. Insubordination or mutiny met instant and violent punishment.

Newton shared in the brutality against his fellow creatures. If naval life had been brutal it was for a high cause. The Slave Trade was for gain, and in 1745 not a pen nor a tongue had questioned or condemned it. In old age John Newton revealed what it had done to his character as a young man when he told a Committee of the Privy Council, from his own experience, that he knew no method of getting money which had so direct a tendency to efface the moral sense, to rob the heart of every gentle and humane disposition and to harden it like steel.

About a third of the cargo was female. As black women and girls came on board, naked, trembling, terrified, almost exhausted with cold, fatigue and hunger, they were exposed to the wanton rudeness of the crew. The poor creatures could not understand English, but looks and manner were sufficiently intelligible as in imagination the prey was divided upon the spot for future use.

John Newton let lust run unchecked. His heart lay with Polly but his body refused to be denied. Since the women were kept on deck at liberty in daytime, a seaman's opportunity came easily and he need ask no consent, since resistance or refusal would be in vain. Sometimes, he might take one at night while on duty, for owing to the heat and filth the crew went naked in the holds where the women lay, equally naked, and discipline could not restrain desire, especially before the holds grew crowded. Any consequence would be born far away in the sugar islands, perhaps adding to the profit of the voyage. It is a curious fact that there may be American or Caribbean blacks in whose veins runs the blood of John Newton.

Newton later referred to a Scripture verse which he said aptly described his activities at this time' *2 Peter 2: 14*. It begins, 'Having eyes full of adultery, and that cannot cease from sin.' He was a lecher. Yet his wickedness, as he later saw it, was not of the flesh only. In his mind and soul he was a militant atheist, and the verse continues: *'beguiling unstable souls.'* John Newton ridiculed faith and morals and took special delight in destroying any vestiges of religion which he detected in crew members.

Nine years later, in the earliest account of his Christian conversion (a letter to Dr. Jennings) he wrote an uninhibited pen portrait of himself at this time: 'That I was a slave to every customary vice was perhaps the lightest part of my character. My obstinate contempt of the glorious gospel, and the horrid effrontery with which I treated it, distinguished me even amongst freethinkers themselves before I had reached the age of 20; and so industrious was I in propagating my tenets that I believe for some years I never was an hour in any company without attempting to corrupt them.

'Methinks I had rather borne the infamous character of a thief, then I could perhaps have made restitution; but now, however wonderfully the Divine forgiveness may be vouchsafed to me, I fear there are too many will have lasting reason to bewail the day in which they first become acquainted with me.'

One of these was the captain of the slaver. He was not at all religious and did not dislike wickedness except where it damaged his own interests but he much regretted on personal and professional grounds the exchange he had made at Madeira. Newton had grown careless, disobedient, even mutinous at times, stirring other members of the crew to dangerous escapades.

The captain's temper flared hot and so did Newton's. They flew into furious arguments. Worse, Newton made fun of him. In revenge for some imagined slight Newton applied his wit, and a skill at turning verses, to the making of a song which, without naming names, ridiculed the captain, in his ship, his plans and his person. Newton could sing well. He taught the song to the whole ship's company, and thus he repaid kindness and protection. Only respect for the boy's father stayed the captain's hand from punishing such insubordination; he had the legal right and the power to make life very unpleasant for an object of his anger.

The mate of the ship also hated Newton, who tasted his temper and quarrelled with him. At the turn of the year 1745–46, when the holds were crammed with slave cargo and the ship lay in the Rio Nuna, the usual northerly boundary of the Trade, preparing for the Middle Passage, the captain died. The mate succeeded to the command.

Newton at once realized his danger. The new captain cared nothing for the father whom the dead man had respected, and as soon as the ship reached the West Indies he would take the first opportunity of putting Newton on board a man-of-war, and 'this, from what I knew already was more dreadful to me than death.'

Newton resolved to quit and to try his fortune in Africa. He asked Clow, who was about to land and continue his trading, for permission to enter his service. Clow agreed; Newton dreamed such golden dreams that he did not take the precaution of asking for a contract. The new captain consented and for six months' wages gave a bill on the owners in England, a worthless scrap of paper as it proved, since they went bankrupt.

6
Captivity

Clow had determined to develop a fresh factory. He took
Newton to the largest of three small sandy in-shore islands
covered with coconut palms and plantains (banana trees)
and known to traders as the Plantains. The islands lay some
twenty leagues south of a river mouth guarded by a
mountainous peninsula which gave the river its name: Sierra
Leone, Lion Mountain.

The Plantains were uninhabited. Clow judged that their
location might afford him a prime market. Using slaves
bought at the factory a few leagues away on the Benanoes,
he and Newton made themselves a commodious place. The
buildings, of coconut logs thatched with banana leaves,
included a central homestead for living rooms, smaller huts
for sleeping and kitchen, and shelters for the merchandise,
whether deadstock such as knives, guns, rum and other
imports, or the livestock – the slaves which they would
export as native chiefs made their way in for trade. John
Newton determined to retrieve lost time and be diligent,
and the new factory thrived; it worried him not at all that
his traffic was in human flesh. He laid aside his contentious-
ness as an atheist, for Clow had long abandoned pretensions
to religion and thus offered no scope for argument or
ridicule.

When the Plantains had become thoroughly habitable
Clow left Newton in charge and sailed away several hundred
miles north to collect his woman. Newton had learned

already that she was a princess of her tribe and that Clow's early success in trade, and his wealth, owed much to having won her favour. No parson or witchdoctor had joined them together in matrimony but she had learned European ways and when she arrived on the island Clow expected everyone to treat her as the mistress of the house. Her name sounded like Pee-eye, or P.I. pronounced as separate letters.

Unfortunately for Newton, Princess P.I. showed herself prejudiced against him from the first, whether because she feared the influence of another white man or resented his share of profits. She soon had opportunity to do him harm. Shortly before Clow had planned to take him in the shallop (a small, masted boat for river and in-shore work) up the coast to trade, Newton fell sick, and into that misery which a tropical fever can generate in the strongest man, his throat fiery, brow throbbing, body prostrated by lassitude.

Clow gave orders for his comfort but refused to delay departure, and at daybreak Newton awoke to see the shallop sail pass rapidly out of sight behind the palms along the shore. Once Clow had gone, the black princess made herself queen of all his goods and people. Expressing annoyance and contempt for a white man's sickness, though it was common enough, she soon countermanded the orders for Newton's comfort because he did not recover quickly. She had him moved from his comfortable hut to an empty slave shelter in the lines, where his bed was a mat spread on a chest and his pillow a palm log. He could scarcely obtain water when burning with the fever, for the household slaves followed their mistress's lead and openly displayed scorn, mixed a little with pity but not enough to disobey her orders to neglect him.

She hoped he would die. The fever, however, took its course and receded, until Newton, now hungry, longed to attend the loaded table in the homestead but was too weak to go. She allowed him nothing but a ration of boiled rice, hardly enough to sustain life. Then came a day when the princess of the Plantains felt in high good humour and after dinner sent across her own dirty plate piled with half-chewed scraps and her leavings of European-style food. So humbled lay Newton's pride that he received it eagerly with thanks, like a beggar accepting alms.

A few days later she summoned him, though he could still hardly walk the short distance to where she had dined. Newton's eyes glistened at the dishes of good food left on the table. With a contemptuous gesture the princess handed him her plate with its bounty of scraps: a half finished fish, the ruins of her pile of rice and a few plantains which, for a near-starving convalescent looked a meal indeed. In his weakness 'I dropped the plate. Those who live in plenty hardly conceive how this loss touched me; but she had the cruelty to laugh at my disappointment,' and refused him another helping from the inviting dishes. She ordered him to be taken away.

That night he dragged himself to a field behind the slave lines and pulled up roots. He did not dare carry them back for fear of discovery, when she would have had him whipped as a thief, but ate them raw on the spot. His hunger left him; then he vomited as if he had taken the strongest emetic. He returned in misery to his bed with empty stomach. Such results almost always followed his nocturnal gnawing of unboiled roots yet he could not resist the urge.

Sometimes native visitors brought food, as if excusing their curiosity about P.I.'s white captive, and occasionally he heard the clink of chains: slaves awaiting export were bringing part of their own poor ration, secretly.

One day the princess paid a visit escorted by her house slaves, to insult him in broken English. She called him worthless and indolent. She ordered him to walk. Since in Clow's absence the woman held absolute power, Newton tried to stagger down the path. She spoke rapidly in her native tongue to her escort, and they began to mimic him, and to laugh and clap, and even to pelt him with limes. He learned to dread these visits of state, not only because of the physical hurt when the escort threw stones instead of limes, without any rebuke, but because scorn from a black, whom any white man in that age despised, was nearly as hard to bear as hunger.

Hunger, contempt, pain, loneliness – in that far country where John Newton had taken his journey, these were the 'husks that the swine did eat: and no man gave unto him.' Unlike the Prodigal Son, Newton did not come to himself. By his own choice, no sweet name of Jesus soothed his sorrows, healed his wounds or drove away his fear.

Clow returned. Newton, stupidly, complained to him in front of P.I. and he did not believe the tale. The awful want ended and strength returned quickly in the usual life of the homestead, but Clow now mistrusted Newton as a liar and when they sailed away together in the shallop on the next venture Newton's miseries had only begun.

At first all went well. Clow knew where to trade, Newton learned fast how to bargain and between them they doubled the profit, so that when Clow's former partner appeared on the river he found the market less attractive. Traders on the Windward Coast felt little mutual love beneath an outward affability, for success by one partnership spelt failure to a rival. This may explain what happened.

One afternoon Newton worked on board the shallop, sorting, checking and making up lots: on this journey they did not ship any slaves they bought. Clow was on shore, drinking with his crony. He returned at dusk in a fury and accused Newton of cheating him by stealing foods at night or when he was away; his old associate had warned him. Newton indignantly denied defrauding him in the smallest matter: 'This was the one vice I could not be justly charged with.' He might be a lecher, with the virility of a young body, and a swearer who could blaspheme with the conviction of an infidel; but the only remnant of a good education that he could boast of was honesty. In whatever he had

58

been trusted he had stayed true, although P.I.'s treatment would have been excuse enough for getting a little back.

Clow refused to listen, refused to produce evidence. He condemned Newton unheard and threw him out of the cabin. Next morning, after a hard night on the deck planks, Newton might have expected his master to listen to reason. Instead, Clow locked him to the deck by a long ankle chain as if he were a slave. Putting in reach a pint of rice for the day's ration, Clow padlocked the cabin, took the two blacks of the crew ashore and began to trade in partnership with his old associate, who thus easily had disposed of a young rival.

All day Newton endured the sun and the burning refraction from the deck as best he could until Clow returned that night with the blacks. Soon the smell of fowls roasting on the spit in the galley encouraged his famished stomach, but he was to be disappointed: a black, on Clow's orders, brought out one unplucked wing and the entrails, and a small portion of rice for Newton to boil at the deck brazier. The entrails revolted him. Then he considered that they could be bait for fish and he put them aside. After another night on deck, with never a word from Clow who appeared to have sent him to Coventry, Newton's morning repeated the pattern of his first day as a convict in chains: a pint of rice; the departure of master and crew; solitary captivity.

At the slack water when the tide changed in the estuary Newton baited a line with the entrails and fished, and when he saw a fish on the hook it gave him unbounded joy. He broiled, or rather half-burnt it at the re-lit brazier and though without sauce, salt or bread the fish tasted delicious.

The rainy season was near and that afternoon a storm burst on the unsheltered deck. Newton wore only cotton shirt and trousers, with a handkerchief round his head, and had a two foot length of cotton for outer garment. The tropical downpour quickly soaked him to the skin, and though the hot sun returned, another storm at sunset left him in drenched clothes for the night. Clow stayed on shore, dry and well fed while Newton shivered, and starved until the tide turned again and he caught another fish.

Sometimes in those weeks of floating captivity in the river mouths and island lagoons, his jailer stayed away two days and nights and never left more than one day's meagre ration of rice. If Newton caught nothing with the line he tried to sleep until the next tide in an attempt to forget his stomach cramps.

And the rains had come. Newton in middle age ascribed his twinges of lumbago and rheumatism to this dreadful period when, in thin cotton he was 'exposed for twenty, thirty, perhaps near forty hours together in incessant rains, accompanied with strong gales of wind, without the least shelter, when my master was on shore.' If Clow returned he unlocked him in bad weather, so that he could join the blacks in their cabin, but when a tornado struck at night in their absence Newton had to endure the horror alone, crouching against the gunwale through heavy rain, thunder and lightning. Perhaps Clow hoped the boy would die of fright or exposure and thus cancel any obligation of payment for his services.

By the end of two months, when the shallop tied up once more at the Plantains, the excessive cold and wet which he had suffered so soon after recovery from long sickness, had weakened Newton's physique and broken his spirits. But at least he expected release and re-instatement.

Instead Clow took him to the forge. To Newton's distress, shame and helpless misery the blacksmith, while Clow watched, put him in ankle irons. Henceforth he must clank and shuffle with two fetters linked by a chain, as if he were a slave.

7

Servant of Slaves

The head slave put Newton to planting a lime grove. The plants were small as gooseberry shoots, to be placed in lines by the hundred, a backbreaking job. Like the slaves, he was made to work nearly naked and the sun burned his body: perhaps the overseer wanted to make him a black. Inwardly too he burned — with shame that he worked under the orders of a slave, that he should be 'a servant of slaves in Africa', to quote his phrase of after years; and, what to his mind was worse, the object of their pity. Occasionally a house slave risked the wrath of Clow by bringing across left-overs from the homestead; the ill-fed Newton's gratitude was mixed with wretchedness that he should be beholden to the pity of a black.

The friendly house slave helped in a way even more important. He smuggled writing materials whenever a ship from Europe appeared off shore to respond to Clow's smoke signals for trade. Newton was convinced that a letter home to his father was the one hope of rescue. If the ship's boat approached the island, shame drove him to hide in the woods from strangers, for it was useless to appeal to some unknown officer for redress; the man would have accepted Clow's retort that his young assistant was being punished for misbehaviour by a spell of hard labour in chains. The trader's word, not English common law, counted on the Coast.

Newton wrote two or three times to his father, the slave

putting the letter secretly in Clow's bag before it was sealed to be taken on board according to the custom of the trade. Newton described his condition and begged help, saying, in sincerity, that he would not return to England unless his father sent a message promising he would receive him and forgive. He wrote also to Polly; at his lowest ebb he retained a hope of seeing again the girl whom he loved passionately through all his distress.

Unless a ship were wrecked letters would be delivered after many months, first crossing to the West Indies. That kept his hope alive. Meanwhile Newton kept his sanity. He did it in a manner which afterwards struck him as curious. On first coming ashore he had put in his bundle one book only: Barrow's edition of Euclid's Elements of Geometry, which he had bought at Plymouth. This he used to take in the brief cool evening hour to remote corners of the island, to draw the diagrams with a long stick on the sand. Without other assistance he mastered the first six books of Euclid. Concentration on mathematics made him forget his misery until, all too soon, the sun dropped into the sea and the swift darkness ended the lesson. He stripped off his shirt and washed it upon the rocks and put it on wet, to dry on his back as he slept. Pensive and solitary he would creep back to the hut.

John Newton was brought low, 'depressed to a degree beyond common wretchedness,' as he puts it. 'I lost all resolution, almost all reflection. I had lost the fierceness which fired me when on board the *Harwich* and which made me capable of the most desperate attempts.' About half a century later, in his old age, Newton on one of his birthdays took down from his shelves a specially interleaved edition of his own book, *Letters to a Wife*, and wrote: 'The troubles and miseries I for a time endured were my own. I brought them upon myself, by forsaking Thy good and pleasant paths and choosing the Way of Transgressors which I found very hard;

they led to slavery, contempt, famine and despair.' But not to repentance.

* * *

One day Clow came strolling into the lime grove, the black princess on his arm. They stopped to watch Newton at his labour. After a long silence Clow said, in tones of biting sarcasm: 'Who knows, but by the time these trees grow up and bear, you may go home to England, obtain the command of a ship, and return to reap the fruit of your labours? We see strange things happen sometimes!'

Clow and the princess laughed at the absurdity. And little did Newton think at that moment of ridicule that indeed he would revisit the place just when the lime trees were ready to bear fruit their first season; and that he would come in a condition of prosperity which excited the envy of those who once scorned to let him sit at their table.

The first change in his fortunes occurred quite soon after Clow's unconscious prophecy.

Another trader had set up home on their island, which he left frequently to attend to his factories up and down the coast. He had prospered more than Clow and employed several white assistants. He had offered to take Newton and persisted in the face of Clow's refusal, either deploring the waste of a white or because he had caught glimpses of Newton at his Euclid on the shore and sensed he could be useful. At length, late in 1746, Clow agreed. Perhaps he had wearied of Newton's dying yet was ashamed to keep him in servitude another year, and could not believe, after his own behaviour towards him, that Newton would serve him fairly if restored to a position of trust.

Newton was at once decently clothed, well fed, treated as a companion. The trader entrusted him with the care of all the domestic effects, to the amount of some thousand pounds, on next going away, and the 'sport and scorn of slaves' became virtually master of several until his new master, his new friend returned, to find him restored in body and spirits and his own affairs in good order. Sensing his embarrassment at living on a small island as neighbour to Clow and the princess, the trader appointed him to share with another Englishman the management of a factory more than a hundred miles away, in the Kittam district on the Sherbro river's southern branch.

This river actually debouches into the Atlantic not far from the Benanoes but its peculiar course flows for the last hundred miles parallel to the shoreline like a sound, never more than a mile or two inland from the sea. This strange fact would have the strongest bearing on Newton's future.

Newton became fast friends with his fellow manager. Business flourished, their employer was satisfied. They traded in the usual way of the English on the Coast. They did not think of it as dishonesty but not an article was delivered to the blacks in a genuine or entire condition: spirits were diluted by water; false heads were put into gunpowder kegs so that though the keg appeared large, there was no more powder in it than in one much smaller. Linen and cotton cloths were opened, and two or three yards according to the length of the piece were cut off in the middle, where it was not so readily noticed. They cheated in the number, weight, measure and quality of what the natives purchased, in every possible way, and the natives in their turn, particularly when trading with the English, had become jealous, shifty and revengeful.

The English and the Africans considered each other villains. A black on clearing himself of unfairness or dishonesty would answer Newton with an air of disdain: 'What! do you think I am a white man?'

Yet Newton found them at heart a gentle people with a simple morality, good laws and patriarchal government. Except for the hazard of fevers which took off strong men in a few hours, his treks upcountry brought little danger. He often slept in their towns in a house filled with goods for trade, with no one in the house but himself and no other door than a mat, enjoying a security which no sensible man would have relied upon in the England, and especially the London of 1746, without taking the precaution of strong doors, strongly locked and bolted.

Newton had begun to take his pleasures again on any slave girl he fancied, but as the weeks passed he inclined to women of the local tribe, according to trader custom. Occasionally he grew wistful at the thought of Polly Catlett, or felt remorse for the father he had wronged; or his imagination strayed to the scents and sounds of an English summer in the fields of Aveley. But he no longer pined to return. He believed that Polly would never accept him, and he could more easily bear the disappointment in Africa where he lived and moved like a king, than in England.

The local manners and customs grew on him. The throb of drums, the wild dances of the women in their voodoo worship, the sacrifices of a chicken to ward off evil or secure the favour of the gods of field and river, even the sacrifice of a newborn infant in upcountry villages, began to exercise their fascination. Newton had noticed already that white men long on the Coast would often put more trust in charms, necromancies, amulets and divinations than did the wiser sort among the natives. In the phrase frequently used when a white became assimilated, Newton was 'growing black'. Some three months after release from Clow's captivity he renounced all idea of return to England. He thought himself happy.

Had anyone sung 'Solid joys and lasting treasure None but Zion's children know', it would have been John Newton who would have sat in the seat of the scorner to 'deride and pity' those who 'glory in Thy Name'.

*   *   *

Far away in London Captain John Newton of the Africa Company received his son's pathetic appeal, written in captivity many months before. The Captain at once wrote to his great friend Joseph Manesty, the Liverpool shipowner who years earlier had promised John the place in Jamaica which he lost by overstaying his leave after falling in love with Polly.

Manesty had a ship the *Greyhound*, not a slaver, about to sail for the Windward Coast where John was marooned. He ordered the captain to enquire all down the Coast and to fetch him home. In due course the *Greyhound* put into Sierra Leone river and asked for one John Newton, in vain. Her next port of call was the Benanoes, where men reported vaguely that Newton was a great distance up country. The captain made no further search in that quarter, and Newton might never have heard of the *Greyhound* before she sailed out of reach, had he been still on the Plantain islands. Instead, he was a hundred miles south at Kittam on the narrow strip between the Sherbro river and the sea.

Early in February 1747 he planned a trading journey far inland, and would have left already had not he and his fellow manager discovered that their assortment lacked some goods which might make the difference between moderate profit and considerable gain when bartered for slaves. They decided that Newton should wait a couple of days in case a ship passed by.

This was unlikely. The two men used sometimes to go to the beach in hope of seeing a vessel but at that period the place was seldom touched by ships seeking trade; many passed in the night, others kept a considerable distance from the shore. Newton could not recall one that had stopped.

On the third morning the other Englishman walked down to the beach, taking some of the blacks: if he did not sight a ship Newton was to march late in the afternoon in order to halt the caravan far enough from the porters' homes that night for an early start on the morrow.

As the man reached the beach he saw the sails of a Guineaman. She had already passed down wind but sailed near enough inshore to be worth a smoke signal, always the token for trade. He lit a fire and waited until, to his joy, he saw her come to and drop anchor. He embarked in a canoe and boarded.

She was the *Greyhound*.

Her master and captain said he had almost ignored the smoke, the wind being fair; if Newton's friend had not seen the ship for another fifteen minutes she would have sailed beyond recall. The captain then asked, to the other's astonishment, if he knew a young man called John Newton. When the captain heard that his quarry lived at that very place he came on shore at once.

They were introduced on the porch of Newton's house in Kittam with his black household around him and the porters waiting at the warehouse nearby. The captain gave his news that he had come to take home the long-lost son of his owner's friend. When he heard that Newton would have disappeared upcountry within a few hours he quite dropped his usual phlegm, as he thought how narrow had been the line between success and failure in his search, how amazing the coincidence.

Newton heard him out with indifference. The invitation would have been as life from the dead to a starving captive at the Plantains; but now, free and prosperous, settled for life as a trader, his father's forgiveness appeared a trifle. Home was where he stood.

He thanked the captain shortly and refused the offer.

The captain, unwilling to lose him, spun a yarn, a very plausible account of how at Liverpoool he had missed a large packet of letters and papers for Newton which he should have brought out. 'But I am sure of this,' he said, 'because I heard it from your father's own mouth as well as from my employer, Mr. Manesty, that a person lately dead has left you £400 per annum. And if you are in any way embarrassed in your circumstances I have express orders to redeem you, though it should cost one half of my cargo!'

It was a pack of lies. Newton himself did not believe the bit about the handsome estate, though some modest expectations from an aged relative made him think it might be true in part.

He was about to turn away when a thought of Polly stole into his mind. It awoke a spark of hope — that she might be won after all. Mature deliberation would have reckoned the odds too great but the captain's offer looked a way to her hand.

The captain was pouring out promises: 'You shall lodge in my cabin! You shall dine at my table! You shall be my constant companion without my expecting any service from you.'

Newton did not listen. His mind was made up. He would chuck his hope of fortune, chuck his mistress, his semi-royal status, his libertine life. On the spur of the moment he decided to return home and win Polly.

In after years he marvelled at the touch-and-go 'upon which my deliverance from Africa depended! Had the ship passed one quarter of an hour sooner, I had died there a wretch as I had lived.' Yet without the hope of Polly he would have stayed where he was. He once said to her: 'If I had not known you, perhaps I should never have seen the coast of Guinea. But it seems more certain that if I had not known you, I should never have returned from it!'

8

Atheist at Bay

Nearly twenty years later, when Newton was reflecting on his meekness in captivity, he wrote: 'I was no further changed than a tiger who has been tamed by hunger. Remove the occasion and he will be as wild as ever.'

The *Greyhound* proved it. In Kittam, following his near-starvation when 'a servant of slaves' on the Plantains, Newton wanted to succeed and grow rich as a trader. This aim concentrated his mind and bettered his character. But once the coast of Kittam had fallen astern the effect of idleness was calamitous.

The *Greyhound* traded for gold and ivory; for camwood, which was an ingredient for dyes; and beeswax. The camwood and beeswax would save their lives when the crisis came.

A cargo of this sort took much longer to collect than slaves, and she worked southwards down the African coast for more than a year before turning home. Newton, though a passenger who shared the captain's cabin and table and, as promised, had no duties, could have made himself useful as a supercargo to manage the trading, or, with a little refurbishing of his nautical skills, he might have assisted the sailing of the vessel. A small company of some fifteen or twenty souls, subject to the fevers and mishaps of the Coast, would welcome help and the *Greyhound*'s owner would receive a good report which might prompt him, as family friend, to offer Newton a command.

Instead Newton idled, except for occasionally amusing himself with mathematics. And he fouled the ship by his presence: 'My whole life when awake was a course of most horrid impiety and profaneness; I know not I have ever since met so daring a blasphemer.' Not content with common oaths he invented new ones, so that he was often rebuked by the captain, who though a quick tempered man with the usual strong language of the sea, felt bound, as magistrate to his ship's company, to reprove his passenger's blatant breaking of Parliament's recent Profane Oaths Act. Newton also broke the earlier Blasphemy Act, by deriding the Saviour's name and denying the existence of God. And he tore at such shreds of Christian belief as remained in any member of the crew. He ridiculed and parodied the events described in the Gospels.

Newton seemed his own worst enemy. Towards the end of 1747 his wildness nearly cost him his life. The ship lay in the broad Gabon river on the Equator, nearly a thousand miles south of his place of slavery under Clow. Newton suggested and paid for a drinking bout, to pass the hot steamy hours of darkness. Normally he did not take liquor; his father had often said, when exasperated by his conduct, that while he avoided drunkenness he might still be reclaimed; but it amused John Newton to make others drunk.

Four or five of them sat with him on the deck with a large sea-shell for glass, to win a wager as to who could hold out longest, drinking alternately geneva spirits (that is, gin) and rum. Newton proposed a toast: A curse on the man who should drink first. Then they drew lots. It fell on him and he downed a shellful. He had a weak head for liquor and as the shell made its rounds he rose and danced about the deck like a madman in a blend of voodoo dance and hornpipe, much diverting the others. His hat blew overboard. In the moonlight, to Newton's drunken state, the ship's boat looked close enough for a drop from the deck, with a quick rescue of the hat to follow, and he was half over the side when somebody caught at his clothes and pulled him back.

That boat lay at least twenty feet off, and he would have fallen into the water and drowned in the strong tide, for like many sailors in that period he could not swim and the others on deck were too drunk to have saved him, and the rest of the ship's company slept.

The significance of this 'and many other deliverances', from accident, folly, and serious fevers too, 'were all at that time entirely lost on me'. Conscience lay stifled and silent.

At length the *Greyhound* had filled her holds and could turn homeward. She sailed westwards from Cape Lopez to the Spanish island of Annabona, some two hundred and fifty miles from the African coast, where they laid in provisions, especially grain for bread; poultry, milking cows; pigs and sheep which they would kill for meat; and casks of fresh water for the whole voyage. Her captain intended to make the British Isles without touching at an intermediate port, a very long navigation of more than seven thousand miles, including the circuit imposed by the trade winds.

They set sail early in January 1748. They ran westward across the Atlantic to the north-eastern tip of Brazil with normal variations of wind and weather; then northward, far out in the ocean from the sugar islands and the coast of America, until they reached the Newfoundland Banks, wrapping themselves against the cold of late February, all the harsher after their long sojourn in the tropics. Newton had passed the time in his usual amusements, studying Euclid; writing or singing witty verses; composing new blasphemies. He also read the few books on board.

One happened to be Stanhope's *The Christian's Pattern*, a late seventeenth-century paraphrase of the mediaeval classic by Thomas à Kempis, *The Imitation of Christ*. Newton read Kempis with detachment as if a romance, helped by Dean Stanhope's flowing English: 'While Jesus is present by His Grace and Comfort, nothing is hard to do, nothing grievous to suffer; but Happiness and perfect Peace dwell and reign in my breast. But the Moment He withdraws His cheering Presence, all my Supports are lost and gone, all my Faculties disabled, and every Difficulty insuperable. . . .' Newton did not stop to consider whether this were so. Again: 'So all-sufficient, so delightful, so heavenly sweet is the Friendship and Company of Jesus . . . Consider then how miserable thou makest thyself by placing thy Confidence or thy joy in any other.' Newton scoffed at the invitation.

From 1 March a hard westerly gale pushed the *Greyhound* fast towards home, day after day. The vessel, however, had suffered from the length of this voyage and the hot climate; timbers, sails and cordage were worn out and unfit to support stormy weather.

On the evening of 9 March, sitting with others in the forecabin, Newton picked up Thomas à Kempis again to pass the time: 'Since Life is of short and uncertain Continuence, it highly concerns you to look about you, and take good heed how you employ it. Today the Man is vigorous, and gay, and flourishing, and tomorrow he is cut down, withered and gone . . . Ah, wretched Guilty Creature! Ah, stupid Unthinking Sinner! How wilt thou appear at the Tribunal, or what plea canst thou urge at the Bar of Sentence, to Him who needs no Evidence, but is Himself privy to thy most concealed Impieties? Dost thou know this, and yet go on unconcerned, how shalt thou escape the Terrors of that Dreadful Day?'

A thought, unbidden, flitted through Newton's mind: 'What if these things should be true?'

Such an idea had not been near him for years: 'What if these things should be *true*?' His long forgotten conscience stirred uneasily. But he could not bear the inference, and rejected it. Whether true or false, 'I must abide by the consequences of my own choice.'

He put an abrupt end to uncomfortable reflections by shutting the book and joining in the chat around. When he went to bed they were clean out of his mind. Newton slept soundly.

Suddenly the force of a violent sea striking the ship flung him awake. Water poured into the cabin, his bunk lay awash, and he heard a cry from the deck: 'The ship is sinking!'

He rushed towards the companion ladder to give help on deck but the captain shouted down to him to fetch a knife. Newton turned to obey. Another man ran up the ladder and reached the deck as a second great wave, which would have caught Newton had he not gone for the knife, came in and swept the fellow overboard.

They had no leisure to lament him, nor expected to survive him long. Dark as it was, Newton could see that the upper timbers on one side had been shattered. Sails blew in shreds, the deck looked a tangle of cordage; the ship had become a wreck in a few minutes and to the seamen it was astonishing, almost miraculous, that she had not foundered in those first terrifying minutes.

The man overboard left only twelve of them, following losses in Guinea, to work the stricken ship. Some bailed with buckets and pails; others, including Newton, worked the pumps in pairs. Despite their exertions the *Greyhound* was filling. Had she carried a cargo more usual for the North Atlantic, such as cotton bales, sugar and rum, furs, or tobacco, she would have gone down: the beeswax and light woods of Africa kept her buoyant while the crew battled to empty the water. The wave which had smashed her had struck in the later part of the night, near enough to dawn to give hope that they would see the worst leaks in time. And at dawn the gale dropped a little, though the wind still blew hard, and they realized thankfully that the disaster had come at the crisis of the storm, not in its earlier hours when each successive gust would have blown more violent, whipping up higher seas which surely would have sunk them.

Daylight showed that the rotting of the timbers in the tropics had caused them to start in more places than could be counted. Men not at the pumps gathered clothes and bedding to stop the leaks. Everybody stripped off warm outer clothing despite the severe cold, and over this wadding they nailed pieces of boards.

Newton looked on it all as rather an adventure. As he pumped he tried to keep up the courage of the others, and shouted at his companion, 'In a few days this disaster will serve us to talk of, over a glass of wine!'

The other shook his head: 'No!' he said, and began to weep, and Newton caught the words: 'It is too late now.' Being a less hardened sinner the other had been thinking, What will it be like to die?

By nine o'clock in the morning four hours of relentless pumping in cold and hunger had left Newton nearly exhausted, his courage seeping as he looked around at the wreckage and the slopping of the sea water. He stopped and went to the captain, busy in another part of the ship, to offer some suggestion, which the captain accepted. Newton turned away. As he did so, he said without the least reflection: 'If this will not do, the Lord have mercy on us!'

Instantly he was struck by his words, 'The Lord have mercy on us.' Unpremeditated, this was the first desire for mercy that he had breathed 'for the space of many years'. At once it occurred to him: *'What mercy can there be for me?'* — the ship's chief blasphemer, the loudest swearer, the man who mocked the Lord's existence — *What mercy can there be for me?*

Newton stumbled back to his pump. Again and again icy waves drenched them, until with chattering teeth the two men lashed themselves to the pump itself to stop being washed away.

Scriptures learned by heart and long forgotten welled up from the bottom of his mind. The creaking of the pump arms, alternately pushed and released, pushed and released, seemed to merge into a terrible antiphony from the Book of Proverbs, taught at his mother's knee:

> Because I have called,
>> *And ye refused*;
> I have stretched out my hand,
>> *And no man regarded*;
> But ye have set at nought all my counsel,
>> *And would none of my reproof*:
> I also will laugh at your calamity;
>> *I will mock when your fear cometh* . . .

The next wave poured over Newton's head, leaving sparkles of ice on his beard and his waterlogged clothing. The Book of Proverbs engulfed him too: 'I will mock when your fear cometh,' he recalled involuntarily from the depths of memory. 'When your fear cometh as desolation, and your destruction cometh as a whirlwind, when distress and anguish come upon you.'

They resumed pumping and the awful antiphony would not leave Newton alone as that first chapter of Proverbs drove into his mind:

> Then shall they call upon me,
>> *But I will not answer*;
> They shall seek me early,
>> *But they shall not find me*:
> For that they hated knowledge,
>> *And did not choose the fear of the Lord*:
> They would none of my counsel:
>> *They despised all my reproof.*

9

The Hour I First Believed

On that unforgettable 10 March, a day which, for the rest of his life, he never allowed to pass without recalling the year 1748, Newton continued to pump with waning energy until nearly noon.

He would see an immense body of water about to overwhelm their stern; if he looked forward, a chasm, equally dangerous, yawned ahead. The ship plunged. In a twinkling of an eye she crested the other side before the watery mountain behind could catch her. Newton had suffered storms often enough, though never in the North Atlantic, and knew that a vessel in good trim would run over these watery hills and dales for days or even weeks in a gale. But the *Greyhound* was broken and awash; every time she dropped into the next valley he feared she could rise no more and they would all go to the bottom.

He now dreaded death, for he thought at the time that 'if the Christian religion was true I could not be forgiven.' Almost he wished that the end would come so that he could know the worst. Yet he remained only half-convinced that the Scriptures were true. His mood alternated between impatience and despair.

At noon he could pump no more. He went below and lay exhausted on his bunk for an hour until ordered on deck again. When the captain saw that he was useless for pumping he told him to take the helm. For eleven hours until midnight, with one break for food, John Newton steered the ship.

The comparative calm and isolation of the half-shattered wheelhouse gave ample time for reflection. The past floated before him and it was not a pretty memory. He recalled his earnest religiousness in youth, the amazing interventions, coincidences and rescues; his lechery and abandon, and above all, 'my unparalleled effrontery in making the Gospel history (which I could not now be sure was false, though I was not yet assured it was true) the constant subject of profane ridicule.'

If true it was, if Christ had really lived, and had risen from the dead, 'then I thought there never was, nor could be, such a sinner as myself.' Recollection of the spiritual advantages he had contemptuously thrown away forced on Newton the conclusion that his sins were too great to be forgiven. Scripture passages again emerged from unsuspected depths of memory to appal him, such as Hebrews, 6: 4–6: 'It is impossible for those who were once enlightened . . . and have tasted the good word of God and the powers of the world to come, if they shall fall away, to renew them again unto repentance; seeing they crucify to themselves the son of God afresh and put him to open shame.' Such words so exactly described his character that he concluded his doom to be inevitable.

At about six in the evening, when the last daylight had gone in those northern seas, he heard that the ship was free of water. Therefore, against all probability, they might survive. He thought he saw the hand of God displayed in their favour, and there arose a gleam of hope: perhaps he, John Newton, could find the way of forgiveness after all.

He began to pray. He could not pray in faith. 'My prayer was like the cry of the ravens, which the Lord does not disdain to hear' – the instinctive cry to the Creator from one of His creatures. It was not the prayer of a Christian who draws near to a reconciled God and calls him Father, beseeching His loving protection and forgiveness, because Newton faintly perceived that the God to whom he wanted to pray was holy and utterly just. Newton had broken His laws, ridiculed His goodness, spurned His long-suffering and mercy. How could a holy Judge forgive 'a wretch like me'? – unless a way could be found whereby the load of John Newton's sin be lifted from his shoulders and placed elsewhere; perhaps then he could be forgiven.

Standing at the wheel, looking out at that dreadful sea, he began to think of Jesus, whom he had so often derided. He recalled the particulars of His life and His death, the 'wond'rous cross, On which the young Prince of Glory died,' as they had sung so long ago in Dr. Jennings' chapel. He recollected the teaching he had heard there, that Christ's death was a death for sins, but not His own: Jesus had died, 'as I remembered, for the sake of those who, in their distress, should put their trust in Him.' If it were *true* –

A slight change of wind distracted Newton's attention. Although the gale and seas declined with every hour of darkness the ruin of the rigging and the dangerous state of the timbers made *Greyhound* difficult to steer, and when he returned to his thoughts it was to find an enormous scepticism driving out his hopes. The principles of free-thinking, of atheism, had been rivetted to his soul as deeply as the iron nails which held the timbers to the frame of *Greyhound*'s hull. Having lived so long in arrogant assumption that the New Testament story was false, he could not tear unbelief away at a word and throw it overboard. When, at midnight, he was at last relieved at the helm and went below and threw himself on his bunk, he *wished* rather than believed that these things were true.

He yearned to discover 'how I should gain an assurance that the Scriptures were of divine inspiration, and a sufficient warrant for the exercise of trust and hope in God.' Was there truly a God? Could He be known and relied upon?

Newton dropped into an exhausted sleep.

The morning showed that they had survived the gale, which had slackened, and the tremendous seas, only to face starvation. Fighting the storm and the leaks and the water had given no time before darkness fell to survey the extent of the disaster, but now they found that all remaining livestock had been swept overboard – pigs, sheep, beef cattle, milking cows, poultry – and the sea water had floated the movables in the hold, so that every provision cask had been beaten in pieces by the violent motion of the ship. Except for some cod they had caught for amusement on the Banks, and a little of the pulse used to feed the hogs, they had no more than a week's supplies if rationed severely.

The sails had mostly blown away, allowing only the slowest progress although the wind blew fair from the right quarter. They believed that their position lay about a hundred leagues west of Ireland though in fact they were much farther off. They thought they had ample fresh water because the water casks, unlike the provision casks, appeared to be undamaged. Buoyed by hope, most of the crew forgot the storm and looked forward to being home after all.

Newton watched them behave as he had done himself on a dozen occasions of danger and relief, not showing the slightest sense of gratitude to God. As for him, the divine intervention looked obvious, and amazing. Yet he was the most unlikely person on the ship to receive such an impression. 'I can see no reason why the Lord singled me out for mercy . . . unless it was to show, by one astonishing instance, that with Him "nothing is impossible".'

He spent all off-duty hours carefully examining the New Testament which they had on board, in an effort to discover whether he could trust it; he realized that to profess faith in Jesus Christ when he did not really believe His history to be true was no better than a mockery of God. As he read he came across Luke 11: 13: 'If ye, being evil, know how to give good gifts unto your children: how much more shall your heavenly Father give the Holy Spirit to them that ask him?'

This gave him an idea. If this book is true, he reflected, the promise in this passage is true, that God will give the Holy Spirit to those who ask. And this is the Spirit through whom the whole Bible was written, as Newton had been taught in childhood. To understand the new Testament he needed the inner guidance of the Spirit. He must therefore pray for this, and if the book were really God's He would make good His promise.

Newton was encouraged further when he reached Christ's words in John 7: 17: 'If any man will do his will, he shall know of the doctrine, whether it be of God or whether I speak of myself.' Newton did indeed now want to do God's will, and could therefore claim this promise, 'he shall know.' Since he could not really believe that every event that the gospels described, including the resurrection, had actually happened, he decided to take it all temporarily for granted.

In after years Newton wrote and talked often about his spiritual search on the *Greyhound*. Although, at the time, he could not put it clearly in words the movement of his mind may be recaptured, as this profligate sailor struggled with his newly awakened conscience, and with his past, and his hopes and fears; and with all that he read in the New Testament. The sodden, battered cabin, where he could not resist the sense that the living God dealt faithfully with him, became a place of conversion as real as that of St. Paul on the Damascus Road.

Paraphrased from his own writings in various forms his conclusions went like this: 'The more I looked at what Jesus had done on the cross, the more He met my case exactly. I needed someone or something to stand between a righteous God and my sinful self: between a God who must punish sins and blasphemies, and myself, who had wallowed in both to the neck. I needed an Almighty Saviour who should step in and take my sins away, and I found such a one in the

New Testament. It told me that Jesus Christ was "God manifest in the flesh, reconciling the world to himself". I saw that because of the obedience and sufferings of Jesus, God might declare His justice, in punishing my sin, and declare His mercy also, in taking that punishment on Himself on the cross, so that I might be pardoned.'

Once he understood, however dimly, John Newton believed, and renounced his past.

Immediately he found himself freed of his ingrained habit of swearing and casual blasphemies. It did not return, even in the backslidings and uncertainties he went through before he reached Christian maturity. Newton never swore again.

* * *

In the early morning of the fifth day after the storm a loud joyful cry from the watch, '*Land Ahoy!*' brought everyone up on deck in a rush. They saw an uncommonly beautiful dawn, just light enough to reveal a mountainous coast about twenty miles to the eastward, terminating in a cape and two or three small islands. The sailors hugged and slapped one another, for the landfall contours and position were right for the western extremity of Ireland; if the wind stayed fair, all should be safety and plenty next day. The captain ordered, 'Splice the mainbrace!' Though little more than a pint of brandy remained for sharing among twelve, 'We shall soon have brandy enough,' he said. They ate up the rest of the bread in joy and felt like men reprieved.

The mate, however, stared at the horizon as the light grew. He spoke in grave tones: 'I wish it may prove land at last!'

Had a common sailor spoken like that the rest would have fallen upon him and beaten him for such an unreasonable doubt. Since it was an officer, they fell instead to arguing warmly whether it were land or no. Then one of their islands grew red, the sun rose beneath it, the cape broke up and faded. Within half an hour the entire 'landfall' had evaporated into blue sky – a common experience at sea.

The ship's company kept up courage by telling themselves that land, though not yet visible, could not be far, and their wind continued fair. But that very afternoon this fair wind dropped and they were becalmed. Worse, the next day a south-east gale blew up against them and they could not tack into it because the ship was so wrecked that the captain must keep the wind always on the broken side when it blew strong, or the *Greyhound* would be awash again. Day after day, therefore, she was driven farther off course, away to the north of Ireland and westward of the Hebrides, into seas where no other ship would stray at that season.

Hope faded. They had finished the brandy and bread too soon. One twelfth of half a salted cod was a day's ration for each man. They had plenty of fresh water (as they thought) but not a drop of liquor, no bread, scanty clothing in very cold weather, and incessant labour at the pumps to keep the ship afloat. One man died under the hardship. Yet sufferings were nothing to fears: the cod would not last much longer, the south east gale showed no sign of abating, and the crew would soon face a terrible choice: starve to death or turn cannibals.

The captain, now thoroughly soured, knew why they had met misfortune. He blamed it all on John Newton; it was retribution for the wickedness of his ways and speech. 'I've got a Jonah on board,' he would lament, hour after hour. 'A curse attends you, Newton, wherever you go . . . All our troubles are due to my having taken you on board . . . To my great grief I have a Jonah!'

This frequent mention of Jonah made Newton very uneasy, for he knew the Old Testament story where the storm tossed mariners say to Jonah: 'What shall we do unto thee that the sea may be calm unto us? for the sea wrought, and was tempestuous. And he said unto them, Take me up, and cast me forth into the sea; so shall the sea be calm unto you! for I know that for my sake this great tempest is upon you . . . so they took up Jonah, and cast him forth into the sea: and the sea ceased from her raging.' Jonah 1: 11–12, 15.

And indeed the captain said openly to Newton: 'If I throw you overboard we shall be preserved from death, and not otherwise'!

Newton's conscience underlined the captain's words: he was probably quite right, that 'all that had befallen us was on my account. I was at last found out by the powerful hand of God, and condemned in my own breast.' He did not believe the captain would actually throw him overboard. But a more horrible fear assailed him as the south easterly continued into a second week, driving them ever northward and farther from land, drawing starvation daily nearer.

If, in desperation, the crew decided to kill and eat one of their number, to save the rest alive, would not Newton be their choice?

Part Two

DANGERS, TOILS
AND SNARES

10

'Your Most Ardent Admirer'

On the fourteenth day of the adverse south-easterly Newton was again at the wheel.

Whenever off duty he had crept to his cabin, terrified of a contrived 'accident', from which it would be a short step to the cookpot of a starving crew. He had spent his time reading the New Testament, and à Kempis, and a bishop's book of sermons he had found on board: a sermon on the cross moved him much. He was struggling to pray, not simply for rescue from their terrible predicament but for faith and understanding. 'How faint and wavering were my first returns to Thee.' He had been heartened especially by the story of the Prodigal Son, which seemed to parallel his own; he clung, as an illustration of God's attitude to returning sinners, to the father's goodness in running to meet such a son.

Newton could expect neither sympathy nor guidance from man. All on board would have laughed and sworn, assuming his questions some new trick in blasphemy, although they must have noticed that he swore no longer himself. They shared the hunger, cold, weariness and fears of sinking or starving, but the bitterness of heart was peculiarly Newton's own because no one else saw the hand of God in their past deliverance or hoped for Him in their present danger. Yet as he stood at the wheel on the fourteenth day he knew that for him, hope had become stronger than the despair to which all the others had abandoned themselves. Prayer came more easily. He had dared to believe that God had a particular purpose in saving his soul and therefore would save the body too, and his companions. God had saved the Apostle Paul to display him before the world as a trophy of His grace; perhaps God planned to do the same with John Newton.

It was then that he noticed a slight shift in the compass. As he watched, the strong wind came round to the very point they needed to suit the battered part of the ship which must be kept out of the water. The wind dropped. And when, hoping almost against hope, they set more canvas on their masts, it blew just gently enough for the few remaining sails to bear.

Late March was an unsettled time of year in these seas, yet this gentle, favourable wind continued all the next week without observable alteration or increase and they knew the *Greyhound* headed for Ireland again, though they must husband strictly the dwindling provisions. At last, on the twenty-seventh day since their disaster, the deck heard once again the shout, 'Land Ahoy!' This time it was land indeed, the island of Tory off Donegal. Next day they rounded Dunree Head and limped up Lough Swilly on 8 April 1748. Their very last victuals were boiling in the pot as they anchored beneath Buncrana castle.

Two hours later the wind got up and blew violently. If the *Greyhound* had been out at sea in her shattered, feeble state, they must surely have gone to the bottom.

Thankfully they began to disembark. Then a shout brought some of them running down to the hold. The mate had made a horrifying discovery: the five still untapped fresh water butts, which had relieved the crew's misery by encouraging all to drink plentifully when so short of food, and that food salted fish, were in fact empty. Their backs had been stove in by the storm.

Had the crew realized all along how little fresh water remained, they would have rationed it, and the necessarily short ration would have increased the distress. Unknowingly they had drunk their last drop as they anchored in harbour.

To John Newton the entire episode, from the first storm until the change of wind which brought them to port in the nick of time, looked nothing less than an act of God: 'Thou didst preserve me from sinking and starving.' He determined to make a solemn dedication of himself to his Deliverer.

He moved to comfortable lodgings in Londonderry, the walled city a short distance from Lough Swilly where the *Greyhound* lay under repair, and with Irish food and smiling Irish kindness his health and strength returned. He attended morning and evening prayers at a Londonderry church. The clergyman showed no interest in this mariner back from a watery grave, and when a sacrament Sunday drew near, and Newton, having studied the Book of Common Prayer, formally gave notice of his intention to take it, the clergyman smiled and said that the rubric enjoining such notice had long fallen into disuse. Newton had expected the clergyman to examine him, according to the rubric, as to whether he were 'an open and notorious evil liver', and he would have then declared himself 'to have truly repented and amended his former naughty life.'

However, when the day came he arose very early, and in his room and throughout the service in church 'was very particular and earnest in my private devotion and, with the greatest solemnity, engaged myself to be the Lord's for ever, and only His. This was not a formal but a sincere surrender under a warm sense of mercies recently received.' A deep peace but no ecstasy or thrills of joy accompanied the surrender. Newton used to say that he never experienced the 'first love', the honeymoon feelings sometimes associated with Christian conversion. And his understanding of the faith remained shallow, for he assumed that the terms on which God had prolonged his life were those of a galley slave – an interval for labouring at his duty before being called to account at the throne of judgement.

One duty lay clear: to write to his father for forgiveness.

His father replied affectionately. He had mourned his boy as drowned, the *Greyhound* being long overdue, and now rejoiced both for John's survival and for his turn from evil. The old Captain had been appointed Governor of Fort York in Hudson's Bay and would soon sail from the Nore, while the step-mother and their three children would remain at Rotherhithe on the Thames near London; he promised to take John as assistant if he reached the Nore in time. But John felt an obligation to his benefactor and rescuer, Mr. Manesty the owner of the *Greyhound*, not to leave Ireland until he could sail in her to Liverpool. Two or three affectionate letters passed between the Newtons but ship repairs took long and when the *Greyhound* reached Liverpool at last, late in May 1748, a further letter from his father broke the news that he sailed from the Nore about that very day; his forgiveness in person must wait until after the three-year term as Governor.

Those years would be strenuous, perhaps dangerous – as indeed they proved – for an elderly man; and when John Newton the younger called on his benefactor, Mr. Manesty, he learned to his surprise that they could be strenuous and dangerous for himself too.

There must have been some quality in Newton which commanded the instant respect of a stranger; this, with the report which the *Greyhound*'s captain had doubtless given of Newton's new reliability and his seamanship, together with the strength of old friendship for his father, prompted Manesty, on first setting eyes on the young man who had caused him past disappointment and trouble, to offer him the immediate command of one of his slavers, the *Brownlow*.

It would have been a prize to lay at Polly's feet, should she permit him to approach her, yet Newton hesitated and asked for time to decide. When he waited upon Manesty again he thanked him from the heart but declined. 'Until now,' he said, 'I have been unsettled and careless. I think I had better make another voyage first and learn to obey. And also gain a further insight and experience in the business of slave trading before I venture to take such a charge.' Mr. Manesty, who was treating Newton almost as a son, understood and approved. He appointed the *Grey-hound*'s mate to be master of the *Brownlow* and engaged Newton as her mate or first officer.

All this time Newton had been in depths of gloom. He had not dared approach Polly. His fornications in Africa had forfeited all claim to this pure girl of his dreams, who would now be twenty years of age. He could not believe she would accept the hand of such a wretch. From Ireland therefore he had sent a letter to her aunt, possibly their previous intermediary when the Catletts had forbidden the young midshipman to write, and had begged her to discover whether Polly would allow him to pay court. He asked for a reply to Liverpool; on his arrival he had found none.

His father, when announcing immediate departure for Hudson's Bay, had told John of visiting the Catletts at Chatham on his way down river and that they gave their blessing to the match, as did he; John now had to obtain only one person's consent. But still no letter. John Newton despaired. He had nothing on which to marry (this was before Manesty's offer) and he concluded he must break it off.

He wept. Nearing his twenty-third birthday, hardened by years of adventure, he wept as he wrote to the aunt that until his affairs prospered he was determined for Polly's sake to divert his thoughts from her 'as much as possible; and though I do not expect to be ever able wholly to conquer my passion, I will endeavour to keep it within my own breast, and never to trouble either her or you any more with it.'

Then came Manesty's offer of the *Brownlow*. Soon afterwards he received from the aunt, crossing his gloomy letter, the news that the Catlett family were temporarily in London and that nothing hindered John Newton paying his respects to parents and daughter. Dipping deep into his slender resources Newton took a place in the London coach. Three or four days later the Catletts welcomed him.

He found Polly a young woman of poise and charm and good nature, with the same simplicity which had captured his heart long ago. She might not be beautiful as the world accounted beauty, but she exceeded all that he had dreamed during the terrible past four years.

But his heart quite failed to loosen his lips. John Newton stood tongue tied, scarcely making small talk as Polly's mother prattled away with harmless questions about an Africa which, fortunately, she could scarcely imagine. The man who had carelessly and heartlessly taken slave women on the Coast, who had kept a native mistress, behaved in Polly's presence like a callow youth.

And she, though polite and kindly as to a long-lost cousin returned from the sea, gave cold encouragement. He grew certain she had no other suitor, for it was not in her nature to deceive, but the passion hammering his heart evoked no echo in hers. As he left, he stammered a request to be allowed to write. She did not formally forbid him.

He returned to his stepmother's house and tried to express in a letter the love which he had failed to declare in Polly's presence. Recalling the many times he had written from the Navy and from Africa he moaned that no one had ever pursued a love affair so long without a crumb in return. In high flown language he begged 'a little of your charity, one morsel for God's sake, before I am quite starved.' The slightest encouragement, he wrote, would afford him intense pleasure without compromising her freedom to accept or reject him. He pleaded that she bestow an occasional thought on him, 'and not too precipitously put it out of my power to show to all the world what I have often repeated to you, I mean that I am with the most inviolable regard Dear Polly Your most faithful and ardent admirer and servant, *J. Newton.*'

Money did not run to a return to Liverpool by coach or even by stage waggon. He walked, day after day alone in heat, dust and fatigue; short of money, without friends. He built castles in the air, persuading himself that he had seen so much generosity in Polly's behaviour that he could hope. However, he decided as he walked that if her reply contained an absolute refusal he would try to conquer or at least to smother his passion for ever.

Her letter came within a day or two of his reaching Liverpool. He kept it for some time before he dared break the seal. When he did, O joy! She was kind. She wrote in most cautious terms but it was much in his favour that she wrote at all, and had not sent through her mother a formal rejection of his advances. She knew that he would take her letter like this. He was sure she was too honourable and good to trifle with him after he had placed the affair in a serious light.

Solemnly he resolved to be worthy of her in character and in fortune, and so serve God too. On that high note he set sail in the *Brownlow*. Little did he know what the Slave Trade would do to his resolves.

11

'The Dreadful Effects of the Trade'

The lamps of the anchored *Brownlow* cast their reflection on the dark waters of a West African estuary north of Sierra Leone. Leaning on the gunwale her mate, John Newton, could see the fires of the native village whence he had brought back a batch of women slaves: he had bargained successfully with the local chief and they were now stretched out in the holds which already began to fill nicely with males and females.

Distant drumbeats stirred his blood as they had stirred it on the Sherbro before his return to England. He fought against his feelings, but not too hard. All the way from Liverpool he had slipped little by little from the Christianity he had embraced. Everyone would expect, he once wrote, that after 'such a wonderful unhoped-for deliverance', and after his eyes had been to some extent opened, he would 'immediately cleave to the Lord and His ways . . . But alas! It was far otherwise with me'.

On the outward voyage he slackened in prayer, forgot to read his Bible, cooled his gratitude for past mercies, until by the time the *Brownlow* arrived on the Coast 'I was almost as bad as before', except that his lips were free of swearing, blasphemy and 'contempt of God's word and commandment', as the Anglican litany puts it. He had lacked any human support in his pilgrimage. No brother Christian served on board, for in 1748 they were rare birds indeed among seamen. His short sojourn in Liverpool had brought him no pastor, for in those early days of the Evangelical Revival true pastors too were rare. Above all he suffered from what he himself would afterwards describe in his evidence before the Privy Council as 'the dreadful effects of the Slave Trade on the minds of those who engage in it'.

When he had shipped the slaves that afternoon he had seen the salacious eyes which the seamen cast over the naked bodies of the black girls at the inspection, and knew that each man had chosen his fancy. Newton had stifled his lust then, but now the native drums ashore were beating a quickening tempo which maddened him with desire. He fought it feebly, then hurried down to the hold and raped a girl.

Thereafter he 'followed a course of evil of which, a few months before, I should not have supposed myself any longer capable. I was fast bound in chains, I had little desire and no power at all to recover myself.' Whenever his conscience smote him, temptation proved the stronger. As in most slavers, the *Brownlow*'s captain allowed officers and men unlimited licence. Provided they carried out properly the ship's business of sailing and trading, they might do as they pleased with the women cargo, although he knew that these excesses contributed to the loss of seamen by infecting them, or weakening them against fevers until lewdness ended in death.

And so it nearly was with John Newton.

About a month after arrival in Guinea the captain sent him in the longboat to sail from place to place to buy slaves. At length he reached the Plantain islands and revisited, 'in easy circumstances' just as Clow had predicted in sarcasm, the scene of his captivity, pain and disgrace. Clow received his former slave with respect; Princess P.I. and others who had despised him were now his flatterers; the limes he had planted when in chains had grown tall and promised fruit for the following year when he might be back in command of a ship.

Newton took it all for granted, with no thought of amazing grace or memory of the storm. He lorded it with exquisite politeness over Princess P.I., treated Clow with familiarity, and the blacks, who had pitied him in his extremity, with disdain.

Clow provided him with a black girl for his pleasure, for this was a normal hospitality on the Coast. And so it might have gone on, with John Newton lost to history, had he not suddenly fallen ill of a violent fever, 'which broke the fatal chain and once more brought me to myself.' He lay wracked, throbbing, thirsty in the very room where he had watched Clow sail away at the start of the ill-treatment at P.I.'s hands. Death now summoned him, as he thought, and when he faced the prospect his heart smote him as he recalled the dangers and deliverances of the past, his earnest prayers in the time of trouble, his solemn vows before the Lord at that Holy Communion service in Ireland, and his subsequent ingratitude for all God's goodness. He began to wish that he had been allowed to drown when he first found mercy: perhaps the *Greyhound*'s captain should have thrown him overboard after all.

Despair overwhelmed him. He had crucified the Son of God afresh and thus had shut and locked the door of hope. Then he remembered that his Judge was a Father of infinite mercy and tenderness.

Weak, almost delirious, Newton rose from bed and crept to a remote corner of the island. Between the palm trees and the sea he knelt upon the shore and found a new liberty to pray. He dared not make any more resolves but cast himself before his Lord, who should do with him as He pleased. No particular text or shaft of spiritual light flooded his mind but he was able to hope and believe in a crucified Saviour. The burden fell from his conscience. Peace returned, and from that hour his health improved so fast that when he returned to the ship two days later he was well.

This was a turning point as decisive as the storm of the previous spring.

Never again did he fall right away. Prayer became a habit. And the memory of that black time reminded him often in after years 'What a poor creature I am in myself, incapable of standing a single hour without continual fresh supplies of strength and grace from the fountain-head.'

During the next six or seven months Newton commanded the long boat which sought out black cargo in creeks and shores, and villages up river, wherever a factor or a chieftain had a body or two to sell.

Sometimes he must venture in a little canoe through mountainous seas, sometimes travel through the bush, in danger from wild beasts and much oftener from the more wild inhabitants, who, not surprisingly, seemed to the slave traders to be cruel, treacherous and watching opportunities for mischief. Scorched by the sun in daytime and chilled by dews at night, since an open boat allows no proper shelter, he and his crew would be five or six days together without a dry thread about them, sleeping or waking. Even in the fair season brief storms of wind, thunder and heavy rain were frequent, while in March 1749 Newton wrote to Polly: 'Every day the weather grows worse: violent squalls of wind and prodigious thunder and lightning are bringing in by degrees the heavy rains which last almost incessantly from about the end of this month until August.'

Newton told her: 'Providence has preserved me safe through a variety of these scenes since I saw you last and I hope will continue so to do.' He wrote without irony when he ascribed his preservation to Providence, for if, in 1749, thoughtful men of God had not yet realized the iniquity of the Slave Trade, a sailor making his first stumbling steps in the Christian life could hardly be expected to think of himself as engaged in crime. And certainly there seemed to be several occasions when an unseen Hand interposed on his behalf.

One occurred when the *Brownlow* lay in the Rio Cesters, getting ready to sail for the West Indies with its cargo of blacks. Newton was bringing in wood and water daily by the longboat. He would go up river in the afternoon with the sea breeze, supervise the loading, sleep on shore and return with the land wind next morning. The old longboat, however, was now almost unfit for use. One day when the task was nearly completed he had dined on board and taken his place in the boat. They were about to let go the ropes when the captain came up from the cabin and called down that Newton should return on board. He expected further orders, but the captain said: 'I have taken it into my head that you shall remain today in the ship,' and ordered another to go.

Surprised, Newton asked why, for the longboat never went without him. The captain could give no reason except that he had taken it into his head.

Next morning a native canoe brought news that the longboat had sunk that night in the river: the substitute was drowned. Newton was much struck by this Providence, and the captain, a man of no religion, could not help being affected. 'I had no other reason for countermanding you,' he said with awe, 'but that it came suddenly into my mind to detain you!'

Again, far out in the South Atlantic during the Middle Passage, Newton might have lost his life, for one morning the male slaves rose against their captors when brought up for air and exercise. Those purchased early in the voyage down the Coast had been cooped on board for much of a year and were desperate.

One unguarded minute was enough to give them their opportunity. For the next violent quarter of an hour the *Brownlow* endured a scene frequently enacted on slavers: the helmsman killed by a blow from a marlin spike which had been smuggled below; the gong sounding the alarm; several of the crew, seizing muskets, ran up the rigging, which manacled slaves could not attempt, and fired into the tumultuous mass of blacks. Three or four slaves were killed before the rest, unarmed, gave up the unequal struggle.

Then followed retribution. In the course of his time in the Trade Newton saw slaves sentenced to unmerciful whippings, continued until hardly a sign of life remained. He saw them 'agonizing for hours, I believe for days together, under the torture of the thumb-screws; a dreadful engine, if the screw be turned by an unrelenting hand it can give intolerable anguish.'

The Atlantic passage resumed its peaceful course. Newton used his leisure hours to re-learn Latin by a tedious method which at least gave him some understanding of the beauties of Horace, and a spice of classical enthusiasm, before he reached Antigua.

Here the owner's Agent gave orders not to land the slaves but to sail on to Charleston in South Carolina. This proved a loss: the men slaves who had been so long on board began to drop fast, their patience worn out, and all told the *Brownlow* lost sixty-two out of two hundred and eighteen souls. At Charleston, so Newton told Polly, he was glad when the survivors left for the slave market, since he felt 'shut up with almost as many unclean creatures as Noah was and in a much smaller Ark.'

12

The Hand of Polly Catlett

John Newton was now an earnest but ignorant pilgrim wandering in a spiritual fog with little to light his way but good intentions.

During the weeks spent in South Carolina while they fumigated and aired the *Brownlow* and then loaded tobacco and other cargo for England, he had plenty of leisure. He wanted to know God better but 'my views of Christian truth', he would tell his friends in after years, 'were very imperfect and my conduct inconsistent. Spiritually I chiefly depended on myself: I knew I had been very bad, I had a desire to be better, and thought I should in time make myself so.'

He supposed all who attended public worship to be good Christians and that whatever came from the pulpit must be good. The sermons of the minister of the Independent congregation, Joseph Smith, helped best but Newton could not understand him clearly. Smith had been George White-field's strongest ally during his Charleston visits and would have gladly unfolded mysteries and introduced ardent Christians but Newton, bold enough on shipboard or in the African bush, shied from accosting a clergyman.

Instead, he would slip away alone almost every day into the woods and fields behind the town: throughout his subsequent life secluded woodlands were his favourite places of prayer. Here he began 'to taste the sweets of communion with God', praying and praising aloud. In the evenings he would join the captain's cronies in the taverns or the theatres, according to the custom of sailors ashore, although his relish for amusements had weakened 'and I was rather a spectator than a sharer in their pleasures.' He had to battle with himself when they headed towards the brothels but next day he would be back in the woods, sincerely seeking nearness to God. His thoughts ran also to Polly, and ran all the faster when the voyage resumed and they neared Liverpool, which the *Brownlow* reached before Christmas 1749.

Manesty immediately offered Newton a command of his own for the next African slaving season. On the strength of this promise Newton wrote to Polly. Receiving a kind though non-committal reply he hurried south. At Rotherhithe he found that his stepmother had a friendly invitation from the Catletts to accompany him; she was unwell but sent his young half-brother Billy along as a mark of her approval.

It was seven years since John Newton had fallen in love with Polly Catlett and now he was back at Chatham. Her family tactfully left him alone to press his suit.

His love had not abated. In Polly he saw innocence and gentleness in a world which, for him as a slave trader, was filled with deceit and violence. She was pure; only for Polly could he conquer lust. Her love would be his calm harbour where his restless, homeless spirit could anchor, to enjoy again the sunshine which had gone out of his life when his mother died.

Polly was not very literate. Her few letters which survive are too stilted to reveal much of her character. Newton speaks of her as easy and accomplished in the domestic arts and social graces and much esteemed by her genteel friends; her one portrait shows a cheerful, rounded face with laughing eyes. Yet she remains a shadowy character; posterity cannot well fathom what Newton saw in her on that winter day as he faced her awkwardly, after all those years apart, to ask her to marry him.

And Polly said, 'No.' Moreover, she said he must not raise the matter again, and she said this with so grave a face that he nearly took her refusal as final.

He withdrew to a wood nearby and walked up and down a leafy ride. Sure that no one was within hearing he spoke his thoughts aloud, considering how he might best deserve and return Polly's love and praying for her welfare. In the days to follow he had many tender soliloquies in the wood and often repeated her name, just to hear it returned by the echo from the trees.

Her kindly aunt who lived near, and had been the first channel of his love, encouraged him to persist. The whole Catlett family smiled on his efforts. One day her mother, probably as deliberate encouragement, let slip that Polly had remarked, '*If* we should be married, we should do well together.'

After that, John Newton decided to brook no denial, strengthened by his conviction that Polly was too generous to send him empty away.

At evening he touched again the subject on which she had told him to be silent. Again she refused, but he thought she did not speak in so peremptory a manner. He persisted. In a little time she heard without interrupting him, and then proceeded to argue and object in a cool, conversational way. She told him he pressed her to a life in which, as Mrs. John Newton, she would often look back with regret to 'happy Polly Catlett'. He tried to persuade her that she would not lose her pleasures, only change them.

Remembering a line from a play, 'The woman that deliberates is *gained*,' he began to urge his point more closely, until she yielded! She gave her hand in token of consent. And John, who had been for so long begging for it, could only take it in trembling and surprise, thinking he must be dreaming. He sat stupid and speechless, minute after minute, until she showed her embarrassment. His heart fluttered to such a degree that he could not get a word out.

That night he fell asleep in perfect contentment, aware as never before how strongly he loved her.

They were married on 1 February 1750. Reaction set in at once. He wondered whether he had made a mistake. Eager for heights of emotion yet diffident and awkward, while Polly was so cautious and reserved that she seemed hardly the Polly of his dreams, John Newton passed some uncomfortable weeks. Then, as he put it afterwards to Polly, 'the prospect cleared up and by quick stages I attained to that consciousness of your affection which I would not exchange for empire and the riches of the whole globe.'

The both fell deeply and irrecoverably in love. Her constant endearments loosened his tongue. 'Love cannot be ardent and intense until it becomes reciprocal,' he would say. John and Polly, still living under her parents' roof, became wrapped up in one another all day long, and when John lay in her arms at night he would silently reflect how different this was 'from the vice the libertine would disguise under the name of love', which he had tasted too often on the Coast.

They were so happy together that he began to lose his ambition to serve God. Had this matrimonial bliss continued he might have sunk without trace as a Christian. To paraphrase his comments: 'Any spiritual light I had was like the first faint streaks of early dawn; and I believe it was not yet day-break for my dear wife. She was not lacking in polite religion but knew nothing of a pilgrimage of faith. We were like two inexperienced people on the edge of a wild wilderness, without a guide, ignorant of the way they should take, entirely unaware of the difficulties they might encounter. My faint sense of dependence on God was wearing away and I was too much a coward to dare pray aloud with Polly. Christ had begun to knock at the door of my heart; if he had not mercifully determined to take no denial, my idolatrous attachment to her would I believe have barred and bolted him out.

'He designed a separation which, though very grievous to me, proved the means of drawing us both to himself.'

The African sailing season approached. Newton had been disappointed in his expectation of some family income soon after his marriage, which would have enabled him to abandon the sea and set up in a landsman's calling. With no other support for Polly he must take up his command. 'The prospect of the separation was as terrible to me as death.' In a bid to prevent it he began to gamble: he bought tickets in the Lottery. He spent more than he could afford, all the while attempting to bribe God by promising to give away a good slice of any prize. But winnings never came. All his tickets proved blanks; he ended seventy pounds in debt.

On 18 May 1750 he rode away from Chatham. The Newtons' hearts were too full to say much at parting. John had a good horse, a good road and wanted no company except the charm of happy memories. He would try to cheer himself with the thought of reunion at last, though the voyage might last a year or more.

In the event, reunion came soon. Manesty said he had no ship good enough yet for Newton and kept him on hand at Liverpool, then sent him to London on business and allowed him a week's leave afterwards. The delight of being with Polly again ended in their second parting. And this might have been the last, and Polly a widow, for on the final day of his return ride he was within a few miles of Liverpool at dusk. His horse was tired and thirsty. Newton saw what he thought was a pond a few feet below the roadside and made for it – whereupon horse and rider plunged head over heels into a marlpit. Both escaped unhurt but he heard afterwards that three people had been killed that way. Once again he saw the hand of God.

But all these deliverances were negative. As yet, he had done nothing beautiful for God. He had been saved from sinking and starving on the *Greyhound* by Divine intervention, as he was sure. He had been saved from wild animals and violent Africans; he had been saved from drowning on several occasions when landing or embarking in native canoes which the surf overturned.

And during these years he had been saved, morally, from ensnaring himself beyond hope of reclaim.

He was now nearly twenty-five years of age. It was time to be up and doing if only he could discover the way. He wrote to his mother's old pastor, Dr. Jennings, the friend of long ago. Jennings replied that he hoped to be in Liverpool but Newton sailed first — back to the Slave Trade in the line of duty, and in his first command, the *Duke of Argyle*.

No bystander watching him embark would have prophesied that one day he would be renowned as evangelist, pastor and hymn writer. And had some seen that future, they would have been hard put to guess by what route and through what adventures this uncertain Christian, Captain John Newton the younger, would make his spiritual landfall.

13

Slaver Captain

Even before he had reached Africa John Newton's ship proved a disappointment. The *Duke of Argyle* was a two masted 'snow' (somewhat similar to a brig) of a hundred and forty tons, an old and crazy vessel which he reckoned hardly fit to lie in a dock or make a river passage. Her state added to the dangers of a Guinea voyage, which Newton described as 'a complicated precarious affair'.

The crew of thirty were the usual 'set of wretches'; Newton wrote that he could 'hardly go on board a vessel but I am told, there never was such a set of wretches . . . Debauchery, profaneness and insensibility dreadfully abound in every ship.' He knew the need to keep strict discipline, 'as absolute in my small dominion, except for power of life and death, as any potentate in Europe'. In port there would be a 'mighty bustle of attendance' when he left the ship and a strict watch kept lest he return unawares and not be received in due form. No one might sleep until he was back on board, so he was careful not to stay late on shore without good cause. This was unusual tact in a ship's master but Newton kept in mind what his situation had been on board H.M.S. *Harwich*, and that in Africa he had been 'a servant of slaves'.

He sought to do his duty by the common sailors 'without oppression, ill language or abuse', though his was a turbulent crew. His mate, Bridson, supported him well. Down the coast of Guinea Bridson commanded the longboat, searching out slaves for sale (as Newton had searched when mate of the *Brownlow*) with much gain to the business of the ship until he died of fever. The second mate was a good man and the surgeon, Robert Arthur, became a dear friend, but the bosun had to be put in irons on occasion to teach him a lesson.

One of the worst of the sailors was a fellow named William Lees; combating his insolence and wildness undoubtedly helped to form John Newton's character.

Lees first came to notice at the Sierra Leone river. He refused to keep his watch one night and threatened to strike the bosun who ordered him to his duty. Newton gave Lees a warning. Next day Lees was one of three who rowed a work party ashore but instead of returning on board went without leave to a French schooner and got drunk, liquor being easily obtainable because rum was a principal item in barter for slaves. After their drinking spree the three absconders landed to have a fight with their French friends. When tired of that they attempted to come off against the ebb tide but were too drunk to pull well. They grounded among the rocks and obliged Newton to borrow another captain's boat and send the second mate to their rescue. The mate got them off the rocks but could not shift the boat in time for Newton to go ashore to inspect slaves on offer: the other captain bought the five worth choosing.

Newton ordered each of Lee's partners in crime, Tom Creed and Tom True, to strip to the waist and lie across a gun. He gave them a good caning. Lees was put in irons, since he was already in the punishment book for his insolence the night before. This experience did not reform him: when the *Duke of Argyle* reached the Plantain islands and Newton, not forgetting to look for the limes now growing on the trees he had planted in his misery, paid a state visit to his old master and mistress, Lees gave yet more trouble. Newton had bought a boy and a girl and was about to embark with them for the ship when he discovered that Lees had attempted to desert by hiding on the island. Found, he was drunk and very abusive. Newton had to pay Princess P.I.'s blacks a gallon of brandy to secure him in irons and put him on the boat.

Two days later Clow and his Princess visited the *Duke of Argyle*. One of their blacks who had helped secure Lees came too near as he sat on the windlass and Lees struck at him with the carpenter's maul but just missed his head, grazing his chest, an attack which might have had a very dangerous consequence for the voyage had he struck a mainland chief's servant. However, the Princess permitted the gift of a lace hat to the injured and offended black, which made up the matter.

Newton determined to be rid of Lees. He put him in irons and stapled him to the deck like a recalcitrant slave. At this his two friends of the Sierra Leone drinking spree, Creed and True, became mutinous. Newton decided to discharge all three into a man of war, the fate he had himself avoided by taking service with Clow after being too insolent for the mate who had assumed command on their captain's death, that first voyage on the Coast.

H.M.S. *Surprise* lay in the Sierra Leone estuary. The very next day, running through a high wind, hard rain and a strong sea, Newton took Lees, in irons, by boat to Sierra Leone and delivered him to Captain Baird, who obligingly sailed *Surprise* to the Plantains, with Newton as passenger, and anchored beyond the *Duke of Argyle*. Baird relieved Newton of his mutineers by pressing them into the Navy, giving three of his naval crew in exchange, to their unconcealed delight. Thus Newton, in the pursuit of good order, condemned his troublemakers to the terrors of naval discipline from which he himself had escaped five years before.

Sternness saved Newton from a mutiny on that occasion but on another it was an outbreak of sickness among the crew, which frustrated a conspiracy on the eve of its execution because, in delirium, one of those involved revealed the plans. Newton arrested the ringleader, who had boasted that the ship's company would rise at his word, that he would kill the first mate and the surgeon, then presumably the captain, and sail the ship to a port where they were unknown, to sell the slaves for their own profit.

The voyage of the *Duke of Argyle* did not prove particularly profitable to Newton, who found that his black cargo could be gathered only slowly. According to the custom of the Coast he worked mostly through middlemen who traded with native chiefs for slaves, just as Newton himself had traded before the *Greyhound* had found him. These traders, whether whites or mulattoes, all tried to cheat him except for Clow, whom Newton despised and resented but was obliged often to depend upon, and a mulatto who had been in England and Portugal, fat Harry Tucker; Newton secured his best purchases, whether men, women or children, through Tucker and found his word more dependable than that of any white man on the Coast: he never deceived. Tucker had acquired a great fortune in silver and slaves and lived in state, and the natives feared him because they all owed him money. He had a numerous offspring from half a dozen wives, two of whom Newton took as passengers for four days with their female attendants through a tornado, and soon heartily tired of their company but had dared not decline the honour, as he wanted further trade with their lord and master.

Tucker's son sold him an excellent lot, eighteen slaves, bought from pirates who had cut off a French slaver two nights earlier, murdering six of the crew and driving three others overboard. Tucker had redeemed the French captain. Though Newton was sorry to profit from another captain's misfortune, no man on the Coast would have expected him to have given back stolen slaves whom he had bought for good barter.

As the living cargo increased, so did the menace to the captain and crew of a slaver such as the *Duke of Argyle*.

Fortunately for Newton the captives did not attempt to rise when the ship lay on the Coast, trading, with seven or eight of the best men away in the longboat searching for more. But when at last, in May 1751, the *Duke of Argyle* weighed anchor and lost sight of Africa, and ran well before a strong wind, a young slave who had not been in irons because of a large ulcer and his good behaviour, smuggled down a large marlin spike through the gratings.

A seaman noticed a suspicious action, but before the crew missed the marlin spike and searched for it among the slaves, twenty of them had sawn through their fetters; if they had been left alone another hour they would have risen and brought trouble and damage. As it was, twenty slaves were loose, and the wind blowing into a tornado. Newton could not secure them but kept men at the hatch behind a gun primed and loaded with shot which could work terrible effect in the hold. After a tense night and early morning the wind abated and by afternoon every man was back in irons.

Then Newton paraded the ringleaders, strongly built men who would sell well. He clamped them in iron collars which press upon the neck, jaws and shoulders, and gave them a taste of the thumbscrews, yet not more than to make them scream a little. After only one hour's punishment, merciful by standards of the time, he released them to join the rest below.

These slaves who had tried to regain their freedom were villains in Newton's eyes. Although he now regarded himself as a Christian, and held divine service for his crew on Sundays, an unheard of eccentricity for a slaver captain, he was unaware that he engaged in iniquity. The Slave Trade was universally regarded as a genteel occupation.

And Newton's religious light was still so dim that it was the faraway Polly and not awareness of God which kept him from adultery with the women slaves. More than forty years later he wrote in a private meditation that his affection for Polly formed 'an effectual barrier at a time when superior motives had little influence with me. Though, when upon the Coast, I was always encompassed with women over whom I had absolute power, the thought of the dear woman I had left at home had such possession of my heart that I was no less indifferent to the rest of the sex than a child of three years of age. Perhaps the faint perceptions I then had of [God's] greatness and goodness would not have been sufficient to have restrained me from many evils, which seemed to be easily checked by my attachment to her.' (Other 'African' captains, boasting of their conquests and their prostitutes, had teased him mightily, saying he was a slave to one woman. Newton teased back that they were slaves to a hundred.)

Nevertheless, though unaware that morally he was engaged in a crime against humanity, he was storing up a knowledge of the Slave Trade which would be of incalculable value when the campaign for its Abolition began more than thirty years later. Alone of the Abolitionists John Newton had seen it from the inside, and could recall those days on the *Duke of Argyle* and his later ship: how he had put the slaves below in rows, one above the other, each side of the vessel, like books on a shelf, though he did not have them laid as close as some captains did.

Fettered hand and feet in pairs, it was difficult for them to turn or move, to attempt to rise or lie down, without hurting themselves, and the ship's motion added to the discomfort.

The *Duke of Argyle* sailed on through cloudy dark weather, which was incredibly cold considering the tropical sun, so that Newton had to keep the slaves battened down. When they were brought up to be washed with fresh water they complained so much of cold that he sent them down again once the rooms were cleaned. Soon the weather prevented their being brought up on deck, and the rooms cleaned, every day; the heat and smell would have been unbearable to a person not used to it.

111

Newton recorded in the Log: 'They still look very gloomy and sullen and have doubtless mischief in their heads if they could find opportunity to vent it. But I hope (by the Divine Assistance) we are fully able to over-awe them now.' He had no further trouble, and no disease on board: he buried at sea only half a dozen slaves, a small loss, before making landfall at the British island of Antigua in the West Indies. Squally weather gave him three nearly sleepless nights before he anchored in St. John's roads at sunset on 3 July 1751.

By then the crew had shaved all the men slaves and freed them from their fetters. Joy at this liberty from shackles and from the terror of the ocean was short-lived. Once landed and sold, the hardships and suffering they had already endured would, for most of them, only end in excessive toil, hunger and the tortures of the cartwhip.

Newton never forgot how Mr. Manesty's Antigua agent, who was himself a planter, remarked as they sat at dinner in his mansion at St. John's, that calculations had been made as to whether it were more economical to give slaves moderate work, good food, and treatment such as might enable them to live to old age; or, 'By rigorously straining their strength to the utmost, with hard fare and hard usage, to wear them out before they became useless; and then buy new ones.'

Most planters declared the latter mode cheaper; the agent knew of estates in Antigua where few slaves lived more than nine years.

14

Chains, Bolts and Shackles

Among the letters waiting at Antigua, which included loving missives from Polly in her laboured hand, lay one with news of old Captain Newton's death. The Governor of Fort York had gone bathing; seized with cramp he was drowned only a few days before the arrival of the ship that was to have brought him home from Hudson's Bay. Newton grieved for a father whose gruff affection and constant care had withstood his son's rebellion, and who had not lived to enjoy his reformation.

After five weeks in Antigua the voyage home with a cargo of rum and sugar was saddened further by the death of the ship's surgeon. Surgeon Arthur had been Newton's one true friend on board, with whom he could talk about Polly without feeling he degraded her: the common sailors were unworthy to hear her name. Arthur had caught a fever at St. John's but believing himself convalescent had rejected Newton's suggestion that he stay behind.

The homeward passage in the hurricane season was the most risky part of the voyage as the *Duke of Argyle*, now in a dangerous state, ran before strong westerlies, through cold and storm and high seas. Newton 'trusted to that Providence which has never failed me', and came at last to Polly's arms after fourteen months, in a reunion so sweet that it refreshed him to recall when next under the African sun.

They were at Chatham from the late autumn of 1751 to the spring of 1752. Newton read Christian books, including

113

the classic *Life of God in the Soul of Man* by Henry Scougal, which had been the means of the conversion of George Whitefield, a name which as yet meant nothing to him though Whitefield's and Wesley's revivals had begun to change the land. 'As to preaching, I heard none but of the common sort, and hardly had an idea of any better.' He lacked a guide for his reading, found no Christian friends and, scared lest neighbours and acquaintances think him too pious, never uttered those expressions of zeal and love for Jesus 'which seem so suitable to the case of one who has had much forgiven'. In the phrases of the famous hymn he would one day write about Jesus, he enjoyed 'the music of Thy name', but did not 'Thy love proclaim with every fleeting breath'; or indeed with one.

When the time came to part again, Polly startled him by proposing that he pray aloud. Though he himself could not live without prayer he had been too cowardly to suggest praying with her. They knelt down in their bedroom in the Catletts' home, and as he prayed, Newton 'felt like a person committing his dearest treasure to his dearest Friend', and then went downstairs with a mixture of peace and grief; 'not as one violently torn away, but willingly surrendering her for a time that I might deserve her better.' He expected a long absence; but trust in God cleared away his cares and fears.

At Liverpool he saw his new command, the *African*, still on the stocks at Fisher's Yard, and reckoned it would be one of the best and strongest of vessels, although when launched it turned out to be an indifferent sailor.

This second voyage as a Slave Trade captain took Newton away from England for one year, one month and twenty-nine days. Before embarking he followed the practice (used by Nelson a generation later) of putting up a notice in the churches to interest the prayers of all good people, and to Polly he wrote of God in his first letter after leaving home waters, as 'an ever-present and an all-sufficient Helper'.

During the outward voyage a captain's duties were light in a ship well made, officered and victualled. In the old *Duke of Argyle* he had spent his leisure studying Latin classics; But in the *African* he preferred the Bible. On both ships he spent hours writing to Polly the letters which eventually formed the material for his celebrated *Letters to a Wife*. He used to say that this regular writing taught him style and laid his foundations of authorship.

The months of slave trading on the Coast brought the usual hazards. The outstanding incident was his preservation from an extraordinary attempt to kidnap him. In February 1753 he was doing trade with a white man named Bryan and wished to sail onwards while still owed four slaves to the value of a hundred pounds. Bryan had agreed to hand them over on the beach near his home but produced only two and seemed in a huff. He grudgingly promised to deliver the other two at the same place four days later.

On the night before Newton should go ashore to collect them he had a disturbing dream which seemed a warning of an unpleasant and dangerous experience, with a promise that he would suffer no harm. At first light he took a boat, bringing with him another captain, Jennings, who happened to be his passenger. The surf ran high. Newton had landed in worse, yet he felt a strong inward reluctance to venture ashore. For half an hour he hesitated outside the breakers, then returned to the ship, the only occasion throughout his time in the Slave Trade that he did not keep an appointment. To Jennings he blamed the high surf, but the true reason was a strong sense of a different danger. Jennings made no comment.

That evening the missing slaves arrived on board, together with a letter from trader Bryan couched in violent terms, accusing Newton of misbehaviour with one of Bryan's mistresses, Harry Tucker's sister: the woman had confessed her adultery and was now in chains and Newton had forfeited all further friendship with Bryan.

115

Newton was astonished, the more so when his mate and his passenger both admitted that they had heard Bryan 'talking with such a mixture of grief and resentment that he must believe it; he had too much sense and spirit, too much honesty, to frame the charge himself just to avoid paying a debt. Besides, he was rich; he could not grudge the slaves he owed.' The charge was ridiculous, for Newton had never spoken with the woman, let alone taken her, and it was hard to think who had poisoned Bryan's ear or how the woman could have been induced to accuse herself of a falsehood which exposed her to his rage and a variety of punishment. Newton discovered that Bryan had plotted to seize him the moment he landed that morning, and would have detained him forcibly, possibly killed him. The charge, Newton says, 'greatly threatened my honour and interest both in Africa and England'. It was aimed to destroy his life or his character and would probably have ruined his voyage, had he not turned back in the surf.

At it was, he signed a declaration of innocence and on his next voyage the accusation was publicly acknowledged to be a malicious calumny.

His escape seemed to Newton further evidence of the guiding hand of God, whom he still thought of as a beneficent Providence and a merciful judge rather than as Father and Saviour; the Holy Spirit remained a mystery. Newton did not doubt that the death of Christ was the ground of his salvation, nor deny Christ's resurrection, yet between the truth he accepted and the daily life he must lead lay a fog: he saw through a glass, darkly.

Increasingly he loved to think on these things, to pray and meditate. In daytime the heat of the sun, the smoke of the furnace where they branded and fettered new-bought slaves, and the hurry of trade, were troublesome except when thoughts of Polly interposed. But when the sun set, the fires were out, the slaves battened in the hold, and all but the watch asleep, he enjoyed himself without disturbance. Sometimes he would look back on past mercies, sometimes forward in hope. He would reflect how God in His Providence had been pleased to set him apart, not only from the crowds whose miseries and sufferings were obvious but from most of those who supposed themselves happy. Though removed by a third of the globe from his only treasure, Polly, and though enduring a time of trial, God had highly distinguished him in the three greatest blessings: religion, liberty and love.

Once, on Bence Island, he had leisure for a solitary ramble on a fine and serene moonlit night, when he could pray and think aloud without fear of being overheard. The ship lay in sight at a short distance, which led Newton to recall 'the many interventions of a kind preserving Providence and encouraged me to ask the same gracious protection for the rest of the voyage'. He prayed for Polly, faithful and patient in the prolonged separations imposed by his profession as a sea captain, venturing her first uncertain steps of Christian pilgrimage; he felt that were he master of the whole coast of Africa he would part with it gladly to procure for her the peace he himself possessed, and true comfort from Religion. He prayed that soon they would love God even more than they loved each other. He prayed too for the blacks in their passions, darkness, superstition and loss of liberty.

Again, on Sundays during the Middle Passage, when he would arrange the ship's affairs to make it as much as possible a day of rest for the crew, and lead them in divine service, he would enjoy meditation on the quarter deck or in his cabin. It has been said by writers who dismiss as hypocrisy the subsequent Christian campaign for the Abolition of the Slave Trade, that Newton wrote his famous hymn, *How Sweet the Name of Jesus Sounds*, on the quarter deck of his ship while the slaves languished in their chains below, and that this at least shows his power of detachment. The legend is without substance: the hymn cannot be

117

precisely dated but certainly was written at Olney. He still held too weak a grasp of Christian truth to have written it when at sea.

Yet he would not have seen any incongruity: 'During the time I was engaged in the Slave Trade I never had the least scruple as to its lawfulness.'

This second voyage had not proved profitable because slaves were scarce upon the Coast through over-trading, and the ship's purchases were a violent, liberty-loving lot, probably warriors from an up country tribe who had been captured in war and sold to coastal chiefs. The *African*'s crew was 'much menaced by our cargo'. The slaves' almost desperate attempts at insurrection continually alarmed Newton, and when quiet they were always watching for opportunity. At sea he surprised two of the slaves attempting to get off their irons, and three boys were caught with chisels. Newton fettered these in irons and put them slightly in the thumbscrews which soon produced a full confession. This led to further search and the discovery of knives, stones, shot and a cold chisel.

A month earlier another Liverpool ship had lost the chief mate, three or four white seamen and nineteen black slaves before an insurrection was quelled; Newton, punishing the ringleaders quite mercifully, considered he had been delivered by the favour of Divine Providence.

Two days later he was overtaken by a fast roomy London vessel, well manned and not designed for slaves. Newton boarded her and after much persuasion her captain agreed to take half a dozen of the ringleaders and keep them unfettered, which Newton in his small ship could not. He reckoned that the improvement to their physique would attract a higher price which would cover the cost of their freight.

After this, wrote Newton, 'all the slaves changed their mood, and behaved more like children in one family than slaves in chains and irons, and really were more obliging and considerate than white people.'

Newton had received instructions to land his slaves at St. Kitt's instead of Antigua, and was distraught to find no letters from Polly. He made himself ill with worry, convinced in his ignorance, that God was punishing him at the tenderest spot by removing Polly from this earth, because of his spiritual unfaithfulness, 'especially my backwardness in speaking of spiritual things, which I could hardly attempt even to her'. He thought she might have died in childbirth, for an early letter received on the Coast had hinted of pregnancy. But Polly never bore any children; quite possibly her barrenness may have been a consequence of John's former promiscuous behaviour.

Letters arrived; none from Polly. Newton lost appetite and sleep and expected to die of a broken heart. The owner's agent, Francis Guichard, and his wife showed much concern: good news for their guest was the constant toast after dinner and supper, and a thousand contrivances were set on foot to divert him. If he mentioned anything he wanted, the whole country was ransacked.

At last it crossed his mind to send the longboat to Antigua. A day or two later the boat returned, just as he had sealed his letters, including one to Polly which he had written in a valiant attempt to persuade himself that she still lived to read it. He added in a postscript: 'I gladly break open yours to tell that the boat I sent to Antigua has brought me (Oh, how kind and careful is my dear!) six letters from you, besides several others from friends which, though very acceptable, are of less importance to my peace.' All had arisen from a casual mistake: the owner's change of orders had not been passed to the letter office.

·Newton recovered at once, and sent Polly sweetmeats, and a pineapple which was a present from his hostess. He followed them three weeks later, having warned her that his ship was rather of the slow sort, like her captain.

Then Polly and he had seven weeks together in the early autumn of 1753, the happiest of his life to date, for the Newtons lived at Liverpool in lodgings instead of at Chatham, where they had grudged her family's natural claims. They enjoyed evening walks in the Lancashire countryside, when the setting sun, the trees, the birds and the views contributed to enrich the scene, and as they sat together, facing another parting, their thoughts rose faster than words until the tears stole down their cheeks.

When he sailed again in the *African* on 21 October for a shorter voyage he was growing weary of separations, and had begun to hate being a captain in the Slave Trade. He had not woken yet to moral disgust at what he would afterwards call 'this vile traffic'. Later Newton would confess he wondered 'how I did not start with horror at my own employment'. But no one except little-read philosophers had called in question a Trade which had flourished for centuries; not until six years later did the Philadelphian Quaker, Anthony Benezet, write his famous pamphlet against it and several more years went by before the first stirrings of the early Abolition movement could be detected in England. Universal custom, the attitudes of the day, and Newton's professional interest combined to keep him blinded to the Trade's enormity.

'I am sure,' he would say more than thirty years later, 'that had I thought of the Slave Trade then as I have thought of it since, no considerations would have induced me to continue. Though my religious views were not very clear my conscience was very tender and I dared not have displeased God by acting against the light of my mind. The numerous and continual dangers to which a slave ship is exposed had thrown me into an uncommon dependence on the Providence of God; this gave me a confidence which must have failed in a moment, and I would have been overwhelmed in distress and terror, if I had known or even suspected that I was acting wrongly.'

He had begun to feel that the business was disagreeable. He disliked being a gaoler and was 'sometimes shocked with an employment that was perpetually conversant with chains, bolts and shackles'. He looked on it as the line of life which God had allotted him, and thought himself bound only to treat the slaves gently and to consult their ease and convenience so far as was consistent with the safety of the ship and its whole family, white and black. Yet he was praying that God would soon fix him in a more humane calling, where he could enjoy regular Christian ministrations, and be with Polly.

His prayer would be answered. This third voyage would be the last. It would also change his life.

Its early stages, however, were unpleasant — because his past caught up with him in the shape of Job Lewis.

15

Grace My Fears Relieved

Job Lewis was the clean-living and high-principled midshipman in H.M.S. *Harwich* whom the young John Newton had turned into an atheist and a libertine. Lewis later left the Navy to become master of the *Lamb* in the New England trade out of Liverpool; when they next met their ships were stormbound in company for two weeks off the Isle of Man at the start of Newton's first command.

In the autumn of 1753 Newton again found Lewis at Liverpool, about to sail as master of a Guinea ship, and glad of advice on the skills and perils of the Slave Trade. As in old times they also joked, yarned and discussed books. Newton discovered that the once sober youth of H.M.S. *Harwich* was now a hardened sinner. Confronted, after all these years, with the grievous success of 'my unhappy attempts to infect him with libertine principles', Newton tried to repair the damage. 'I gave him a plain account of the manner and reason of my change and used every argument to persuade him to relinquish his infidel schemes.' Lewis stayed obdurate. When Newton 'pressed him so close that he had no other reply to make, he would remind me that I was the very first person who had given him an idea of his liberty.'

Apart from other factors, Newton's failure to convince Lewis sprang from his own uncertain grasp of Christian truth. 'I once was blind, but now I see'; yet he could not explain the why or the how. He did not abandon the attempt; and when Job's shipowner went bankrupt and threw him on the beach before he had sailed, Newton offered him a berth on the *African* as 'Volunteer and Captain's Commander'. This would provide a knowledge of the Coast, and Manesty promised him a ship of his own on their return; but Newton's object was less to serve Job's professional interest than to gain further time to win him back, hoping that 'my arguments, example and prayers' in the course of the voyage might have good effect.

Once at sea Newton had frequent reason to regret this well intended impulse. Job Lewis was 'exceedingly profane and grew worse and worse; I saw in him a lively picture of what I had once been, but it was very inconvenient to have it always before my eyes. Besides, he was not only deaf to my remonstrances but laboured all he could to counteract my influence.'

As an officer he was so bad tempered and imperious that it required all Newton's prudence and authority to restrain him, especially as the *African* had an almost new crew, mostly of seasoned lags: on the outward passage the ship's cooper and a foremast man broached a cask of ale and filled it up with water, a common trick on the Coast, and stole snuff from the cargo, and were caught. Newton ordered the seaman a dozen lashes of the cat o' nine tails, and the cooper, as a petty officer, a dozen and a half, but in mercy spared each the last lash. When the *African* reached the Coast the carpenter refused orders, grossly abused the second mate, and behaved very mutinously on shore: he got two dozen lashes at the gangway.

With a turbulent crew, and a slow start to the slaving season, Newton longed to be free of Lewis, 'a sharp thorn in my side'.

At the end of December the *African* sailed into the Sherbro river. Newton spied among the shipping a small snow, the *Racehorse*, lying in her moorings empty: she had been recovered from the natives after her British captain and crew had been cut off and killed. The *Racehorse* offered the solution to two problems at once: Manesty's orders were to sail for St. Kitts in April, yet as Newton had warned him, slaves were hard to come by that year, and three or four months gave too little time to barter all the remaining goods from England, which could not be taken onward without spoiling nor be stored on the Coast; he had bought so few slaves that his voyage faced ruin for owner and captain alike. But if he could transfer the surplus cargo to the *Racehorse*, Captain Lewis could take charge of her and continue to purchase slaves and camwood on the *African*'s account when Newton left the Coast. And he would be free of the man.

After two days of sale bargaining, Newton could give Lewis a written appointment to command the *Racehorse*, and a crew, and fit her out with a well assorted cargo. On the night of 18 January 1754 Newton came on board for a last farewell. He repeated and emphasized his best advice, both as to trade and especially as to matters of the soul. Lewis seemed truly affected, for his friendship and regard for Newton were 'as great as could be expected where principles were so diametrically opposite'. He sailed away in good spirits and high hopes.

As soon as he was free of Newton's eye, Lewis put his lust and every appetite on a loose rein. Native women, hard drinking, violent rages, and the treacherous climate, combined to deprive him of resistance when fever attacked about a month later. Newton first heard of Job's illness when the *African*'s longboat returned, shortly after a tornado, with a cargo of camwood and slaves: one of these had been acquired by Lewis, who sent word that he had bought ten more.

Three days later Newton ran the *African* to the point where he had ordered Lewis to rendezvous, and soon sighted her consort. As the *Racehorse* drew near she began to fire minute guns and he noticed her colours at half-mast, a signal that her master must be dead. The officer whom Newton had appointed first mate, Taylor, came on board with the news that Captain Lewis had died of fever four days previously and had been buried at sea. Taylor's account of Job's last days was dreadful. As the fever took hold his rage and despair struck the small crew with horror. He was going to hell, he cried, yet gave no sign that he either hoped or asked for mercy. 'He died convinced,' mused Newton in his sorrow and remorse, 'but not changed;' in the hour of extremity his atheism fell away yet he went to God's judgement seat without repentance. Newton stood all the more amazed at God's goodness to himself, a wretch who might have gone the same way.

A few weeks later Newton nearly died. He had left the *Racehorse* under command of his first mate and set out in the *African* across the Atlantic when he fell desperately ill. For eight or ten days he lay prostrated by high fever, without pains or delirium but on several occasions believing, and the surgeon too, that he was dying. He found himself facing eternity composed and tranquil, his hopes stronger than his fears. 'My trust, though weak in degree, was alone fixed upon the blood and righteousness of Jesus.' The New Testament's promise, 'He is able to save to the uttermost them that come into God by Him,' gave him great relief: he was not afraid of God's wrath. But a peculiar fear greatly troubled him, that amid all the myriads continually entering the unseen world he would be lost or overlooked. 'Perhaps,' he feared, 'the Lord will take no notice of me.' At length a verse of Scripture put his mind to rest: 'The Lord knoweth them that are His.' The Lord might seem far away, despite all Newton's prayers and studies, yet He would recognize the wretch He had saved.

The fever receded. While he convalesced before complete recovery Newton's prayers were dominated by two petitions: that he might understand the faith better so that he could rescue men like Job Lewis, whom he had failed; and that he might be free of his distasteful calling.

Both prayers would be answered.

The *African* had a quick, trouble free run to St. Kitts.

Owing to the failure of trade on the Coast Newton carried only eighty-seven slaves instead of the two hundred and twenty intended, which allowed him to give them more space and to achieve the remarkable record of a passage without a single death: his entire voyage passed without a mortality, black or white, since Job Lewis had died when no longer on the ship's books.

For the last time, though he did not know it, John Newton delivered his blacks to the owner's agent, and thus to the slave market. Then he had much leisure while preparing for homeward passage.

The planters, merchants and other gentry of Basse Terre, the town of St. Kitts, kept up a lively social life to which they invited visiting captains. John Newton, with his good singing voice, his sense of humour and his skill in turning verses was a popular guest in their gracious drawing rooms where house slaves served and picaninnies pulled the fans and the hospitality derived from the sweat of field hands, toiling in the living death of the cane fields under threat of the cartwhip.

At one such party Newton met a lively, cheerful sea captain in his late thirties, and thus about ten years older than himself, named Alexander Clunie, who was not engaged in the Slave Trade. Some 'casual expressions in mixed company' revealed to both Clunie and Newton that they, alone among their hosts and fellow guests, loved God. They walked back to the quayside together and soon became inseparable companions whenever the business of their ships would permit.

Alex Clunie, a Scot, belonged to an Independent congregation in Stepney, near Newton's riverside birthplace and London Pool. His minister was Samuel Brewer, a friend of Dr. Jennings and of the late Dr. Watts the hymnwriter, who had died six years before. Clunie could impart the things of God clearly to a fellow sailor. 'I was all ears,' writes Newton, 'and what was better, he not only informed my understanding but his discourses inflamed my heart.' After their meeting Newton lost appetite for evening parties. Instead, during nearly four weeks in May and June 1754 the two spent every evening on board each other's ship alternately, often prolonging their visits to daybreak. Sometimes on a Sunday, after being together most of the day, they could hardly bear to part at midnight.

Until he met Clunie, Newton had lacked a Christian friend who spoke in a way he could follow. He had learned something of the evil of his heart; he had read through the Bible again and again, and books, and letters from Dr. Jennings, so that he had a general idea of the truth of the Christian gospel; but his ideas were confused. And he was troubled by a fear of relapsing into his old apostasy. But under Alex Clunie he grasped the Christian's security, that he could expect to be preserved, 'not by my own power and holiness but by the mighty power and promise of God through faith in an unchangeable Saviour'. He realized it at last: since he, through grace, belonged to Zion's City, none could shake his sure repose; with salvation's walls surrounded, he could smile at all his foes.

God had given His Son to be the Saviour of the world; amazing grace had saved a wretch and His providence had since interposed again and again in answer to prayer. But Newton had thought of God as a distant potentate whom he must obey. Now he discovered that God could be very near and His love be warmer than Newton had dreamed. Poring with Clunie over the Scriptures in the captain's cabin of the *African*, under Polly's smiling portrait, with the harbour sounds of Basse Terre wafting in, Newton learned that a Christian may claim the Risen Christ's promise to His first disciples: 'Lo, I am with you always.'

Newton began to find (to adapt words he afterwards wrote) that 'the union of a believer with Christ is so intimate, so unalterable, so rich in privilege, so powerful in influence that it cannot be fully represented by any earthly simile. The Lord, by His Spirit, showed and confirmed His love and made

127

Himself known as He met me at the throne of Grace. He opened and applied His precious promises and enabled me to understand the wonder of redemption; He enabled me to cry in prayer to the Father . . . Wonderful are the effects when a crucified, glorious Saviour is presented by the power of the Spirit, in the light of the Word, to the eye of faith. This sight destroys the love of sin, heals the wounds of guilt, softens the hard heart and fills the souls with peace, love and joy; and makes obedience practical, desirable and pleasant. The knowledge of His love to me produced a return of love to Him. I now adored Him and admired Him.'

Newton made an unreserved surrender of heart to Jesus, 'my Lord, my Life, my way, my end'.

Clunie encouraged Newton to pray aloud, taught the advantage of meeting other Christians and urged him to speak for God, whether among the genteel families on the islands or his hardened crew. Until then Newton had never spoken of God, apart from reading the liturgy and lessons on Sundays on board, but had tried to be cheerful always, so that if any among the ship's company realized that their captain was truly religious he would not discourage their pursuit of piety by 'undue severity or supercilious sourness'.

Before they parted, Clunie described to Newton the state of religion in England, with an account of the errors and controversies of the times ('things to which I had been entirely a stranger') and gave him addresses in London where he might gain further instruction. On 20 June 1754 the two friends parted when Newton sailed from St. Kitts, to enjoy a happy, leisured seven weeks' homeward voyage of spiritual and actual sunshine, digesting all he had learned, before the *African* ran into a dangerous, prolonged storm in the Western Approaches.

After almost a week of sleepless nights John Newton anchored safely in the Mersey. He never left English shores again.

Part Three

HOW SWEET THE
SOUND

16

With Every Fleeting Breath

Newton prayed the more fervently that he might change his employment. No answer came: he looked set in the Slave Trade for years. Manesty did not hold against him the failure of the last voyage but agreed the *African* was a poor sailor and promised him a ship almost complete on the stocks; he might even select her name. She would be ready to sail in six weeks.

Newton chose the name *Bee*, and hurried off to Chatham for a month, returning afterwards with Polly. The *Bee*, however, was slow to take wing. October dragged into November. Every day's delay weighed heavier on Newton, like the bolts and shackles of his distasteful work as a gaoler of men and women whose offence was to be black, and captured by their slave-raiding fellow blacks, then sold and resold between blacks and whites until herded into the holds of the *Bee*. He did not doubt it an honourable employment and accepted that the Trade was an economic necessity to England, for all men said so; yet he hated it, and wanted more than ever to be with Polly to teach her how sweet the name of Jesus sounds, and to sit with her at the feet of the saints.

Medical symptoms in the eighteenth century cannot easily be matched with their actual cause, but in view of what happened it is hard not to believe that psychological tensions built up as the day of sailing drew closer, though Newton appeared in excellent health.

131

At last he had fitted out the *Bee*, chosen his crew, taken on his cargo. The *Bee* rode at anchor in the Mersey and in two days they would sail. He left the first mate on board and returned to his lodgings in the afternoon. Polly and he sat drinking tea and talking over past events.

Suddenly Newton fell insensible at her feet. He lay inert, 'deprived of all sense and motion', and she believed he was dead or dying. She kept herself rigidly under control. At her shout for help their landlady rushed in, the maid hurried to the physician, all was bustle and alarm. After about an hour John Newton opened his eyes and they helped him to a sofa.

He regained his senses but the seizure left him dizzy, with a headache and other symptoms which caused the doctors to forbid him to sail. He resigned his command. The *Bee* sailed under another captain for a voyage which turned out calamitous. Newton's substitute died, and most of the officers and many of the crew. The circumstances suggested that whoever had been master of the *Bee* on that voyage would have suffered their fate; Newton's sudden illness had saved him.

Polly and John returned to Chatham to recover his strength, and remained there through the winter and into the spring of 1755. But as Polly's fears subsided she slipped into delayed shock, and while he grew stronger she grew worse, suffering a disorder which no physician could define and no medicine remove. Her husband's concern and her mother's nursing were equally ineffective; and to his further distress Polly still showed no Christian awareness, though she loved her John dearly.

Newton used his sick leave to improve his Latin, French and Mathematics, with an hour before breakfast for devotions. When spring came he took his Bible into the fields and woods and Kentish hills, where the delightful weather and 'the music of birds in the great temple of nature, which the Lord has built for His own honour', helped him concentrate thoughts and prayers and refrain from worry, either about Polly or their future.

He sought out preachers on Sundays but the condition of the parishes around made him wonder, he wrote, whether he had not better stay at home than be present when the glorious gospel was deprecated by those appointed (and paid) to preach.

In June he visited London – and found a new hero. Newton had walked to Gravesend and taken a river boat for cheapness, for unlike many captains in the Slave Trade he had not made a fortune, and savings sank fast during unemployment. The passage up the River Thames would have been agreeable had it not been for the vile company: Newton was obliged to pace the deck for six hours because he could not go below without stopping his ears. He landed near Stepney and called on Samuel Brewer, Alex Clunie's pastor, who told him that George Whitefield had lately returned from America. Brewer wrote an introduction and sent Newton happily onward.

Clunie had already explained all about George Whitefield and John Wesley, how these two Church of England clergymen preached the gospel to great crowds in the fields and the market places, bringing a new breath of vital religion to Britain (and Whitefield to the American colonies) although nicknamed 'Methodists' and attacked by bishops for 'Enthusiasm'. Clunie had described their theological differences and pamphlet warfares, and how the two evangelists were friends again after a period of coolness. Newton had since read Whitefield's published journals and letters, and Wesley's too, and had adored the grace of God in them, but he accounted himself follower of neither.

He hastened into London with his letter of introduction. Whitefield, a florid, middle-aged man in rather untidy clerical dress, with a warm smile and hearty laugh, received Newton most kindly. Busy finishing letters to go to Carolina by a vessel that sailed that afternoon, he could not invite him to linger, so gave him a ticket which would ensure a seat at the Sunday preaching.

Newton rose at four a.m. and after prayer went to Whitefield's Tabernacle, a great shed on Moorfields, where about a thousand people of different denominations worshipped with one heart and soul. Whitefield used the Church of England service, inserting occasional exhortations and encouragements and many little intervals for the singing of hymns, until the spirit and assurance of faith which shone in the evangelist's face and preaching seemed diffused over the whole assembly. They were at it about three hours and Newton went away rejoicing. In the evening a 'prodigious multitude' came; hundreds stayed outside in the yard and many hundreds were forced to go away although the place was supposed to hold five thousand. As Whitefield preached that night a glorious vista of faith and power opened to Newton; Christ was transfigured before him until the young sea captain yearned to love and serve Him to the uttermost.

Back at Chatham he found Polly so weak that she could hardly bear anyone to walk across her room. By midsummer he feared she was dying. He went for long walks in the Medway countryside to pray for her: when faith felt strong he was partly resigned, but often his heart rebelled and he found it hard either to trust God for her recovery, or to submit to His will should she be about to die.

He prayed too about future employment, and in this 'I found it easier to trust the Lord'. The slave coast being overworked that year Manesty would not fit him out another ship until the *Bee* returned, and when she limped home and he viewed his loss he did not hurry into an appointment. Manesty knew that Newton longed to be quit of the sea. An obvious alternative was a post in the Customs and Excise but these, as Crown appointments, needed the interest of a powerful patron. Manesty obligingly tried to secure Newton one such place but missed it owing to an error.

Then came an extraordinary affair which Newton knew nothing about until it was over and a place was his.

Manesty had heard a report that a Tide Surveyor in the Customs, who had just lost his father, had been obliged by family duties to resign. Manesty immediately wrote a request that John Newton be appointed instead and sent it by hand across the Mersey into Cheshire, to old Mr. Salusbury, the innkeeper's son who had married an heiress and for many years had been one of the two Members of Parliament for Liverpool. While the messenger rode towards Shotwick Park, where Salusbury lived, Manesty learnt that the report was false: the Tide Surveyor had no intention of resigning. But the Member of Parliament did not know this when he wrote back promising to name Newton should a vacancy occur. The very day that Manesty received that promise, the Surveyor was found dead in his bed, though he had been seen in perfect health the night before. So the messenger who brought the Member's letter hurried back to Shotwick Park with news of the vacancy and Salusbury, true to his word, wrote at once to the Secretary of State nominating Newton. One hour later the Mayor of Liverpool, a far more important constituent than Joseph Manesty, applied on behalf of a nephew. He was too late: the letter had gone to London and Newton was appointed shortly before his thirtieth birthday.

Newton comments: 'These circumstances appear to me extraordinary, though of a piece with many other parts of my singular history.'

The news reached him when Polly had suffered a relapse. He had to go to London for the formalities and to pay the fees which would secure his place, and took her, with her mother and brother, to seek better medical advice. They all stayed with her aunt. On 6 August she lay in agony with bilious cholic while Newton made his round of government officials, his heart fixed at her bedside in anguish and grief that he must desert her for Liverpool, to take up a post which would be a burden without her, even if she did not love the name of Jesus.

On the second day of his journey north, while the Liverpool coach changed horses at Towcester in Northamptonshire, he wrote from the inn to Polly: 'Before this reaches you your brother will have told you how easy and composed he left me. Indeed I wonder at myself. But the Lord has been very gracious to me and fulfils His promise of giving me strength according to my day. My mind is not distressed. My companions in the coach are civil and agreeable in their way. But I would rather have been alone; for to commune with God and my own heart would be much more pleasing than the empty, amusing chit-chat I am engaged in at present.'

On reaching Liverpool he found that he had charge of fifty or sixty people and was thus a man of substance in the civic community. The Customs and Excise department provided a good office with fire and candles, and a handsome six-oared boat with a coxswain to row him about in style. The two Tide Surveyors alternated weekly between the docks and the river. Inspecting ships in dock seemed virtually a sinecure but Newton's river week could be hard — especially when the Jamaica fleet came in — and the hours dependent on the tides. He must board ships as they arrived in the Mersey, assess excise dues and search for smuggled goods; occasionally he seized some, and after their condemnation in a court of law he received half their value. In summer he might go down river and enjoy himself on the nearby hills while waiting for a vessel to make the tide. Another tide might oblige him to sit in his office until the small hours, reading or writing by his fire until the time came to embark.

A month after Newton settled in, George Whitefield came to Liverpool for the first time. The visit fell in Newton's slack week and he attended the open-air sermon, preached to a considerable but unresponsive crowd. Newton made himself known to Whitefield and next day went to his lodgings for a long talk and heard him preach twice. Then Newton had supper with him and stayed late, for Whitefield warmed to the young Tide Surveyor, saying he had never been in a place where he had so little encouragement, and that Liverpool was the most spiritually unconcerned town, for its size, in the kingdom; which perhaps is not surprising because it was busy growing fat on the Slave Trade.

Newton invited his landlady, an obliging and respectful female, to hear Whitefield preach. The idea so disgusted her that she barely gave a civil answer. However, curiosity or a better motive prevailed and she went the second day and returned very well disposed and borrowed a volume of his printed sermons. On hearing him again she became his great admirer and suggested that Newton ask him to Sunday dinner. He invited four or five Christian friends to meet him. The landlady provided a handsome meal and tried to refuse extra payment, and Whitefield's manners and discourse at table confirmed her respect, so that soon the neighbours called her a Methodist. She bore their reproach and laughter very well, Newton told Polly.

Newton too was chaffed by his acquaintance: they nicknamed him 'Young Whitefield' because of his constant attendance (not, as legend has it, because he was a fiery preacher himself; his own mouth stayed shut as yet). He had more share of Whitefield's company than would have come to him in London in a year. He heard him preach nine times, supped with him three times and they dined together once at a neighbour's, in addition to the landlady's Sunday dinner.

Newton was in a seventh heaven. Whitefield stirred his soul and confirmed his faith, kindling a deep desire to know Christ better and proclaim His love, if a tongue-tied ex-sailor might discover the way. At the least, by testimony and conversation, he could reap where Whitefield sowed by his glorious voice. Liverpool had begun to respond. After

Newton's dinner party they all went to St. Thomas's Square and an immense concourse, reckoned at four thousand people, listened that afternoon. 'The prospect is promising,' commented Whitefield.

On the Monday Newton accompanied him on foot with a small crowd a little way out of town until the chaise overtook them. Whitefield hugged him. The driver cracked his whip and with a last wave from the window the evangelist bowled away in a cloud of dust down the Bolton road.

In the days that followed, many of the poor would accost Newton in the street and ask with tears for news of Whitefield and when he would return. Even some of the fashionable folk had heard him before the end.

Newton wrote a long description to Polly on her bed of sickness in Chatham, longing that the girl who had borne such loneliness and suffering for her loyalty to him should share the comfort of his faith. Not long afterwards he was overjoyed to receive a letter in her own hand. She said she was better. What is more – and Newton could not contain his joy but unashamedly cried praises to God – Polly wrote that she had prayed from the heart for the first time. She had called upon God and He had delivered her. Newton seized paper and a quill, barely pausing to trim it, and wrote back at length. 'Be not afraid, only believe,' he told her. 'The Lord Jesus whom you need and seek invites you, and has declared, "Whosoever cometh I will in no wise cast out . . ." Go on, my dearest. I trust you are in the right way: wait patiently upon the Lord . . .'

Soon Polly was up and about. At the end of September she went to her aunt in London to convalesce and on Sunday slipped away secretly to Methodist preaching – almost certainly the Moorfields Tabernacle. After listening to an evangelistic sermon she remarked to one of Newton's friends, who passed it on, that hearing about the Great Physician had 'done her more good than other medicines'. Newton wrote delightedly to her, 'Well, go on. I hope you will leave

London soon or you will be thought as singular as your husband!'

Her aunt despised Methodists but Polly proved scorn-proof. She was a little afraid that at Liverpool she would be expected to keep company with washerwomen; but he assured her that the few like-minded Christians in a godless town who would be their intimate friends ranked socially above themselves, 'though they do not aim at the top of the polite taste'.

Polly complained that her heart was hard and she would be a hypocrite. John wrote back: 'If you are really afraid of being a hypocrite, it is a good sign that you are not.' To this her reply was charming, and brings her right out of the shadows to take her place at his side as a character in her own right. She wrote: 'I delight, admire, and hang upon every sentence and every action of my dearest John, and yet how wanting, and how cold am I to the gracious Author of all our mercies to whom we owe each other, our happy affection, and all the satisfaction that flows from it!'

This heartwarming correspondence made John and Polly Newton all the more eager to be together again. At last Polly's doctor pronounced her strong enough for the long journey north. In mid-October 1755 she took a seat on the Liverpool coach and John took a seat on the London coach and at Stone in Staffordshire, a hundred and forty miles from London, sixty-five from Liverpool, they fell into each other's arms.

In the past eighteen months, between May 1754 and October 1755, John Newton had passed from seafaring in the Slave Trade to a landsman's post in the Customs; from struggling to be religious to knowing Christ with joy; from lonely pilgrimage to the strength of double harness with a wife who believed. As the Newtons lay in the Bell and Bear inn at Stone they recalled how often they had been restored to each other after long and dangerous separations. They resolved together to declare God's goodness, not merely in secret or to each other but by the whole course of their lives; to love Him more than they loved each other; to commit to Him their dearest concerns and, in every trouble, go to Him who had so often heard their prayers and done them good.

17

'I Will Not Give Up'

One day in January 1756 Newton sat down at his desk in the pleasant house which they had taken in Edmund Street and wrote a long letter to George Whitefield imploring him to return to Liverpool: 'Here are 40,000 people who in matters religious hardly know their right hand from their left.' But Whitefield could not come.

The Newtons felt inadequate as Christians in a godless town. Both of them were still unstable in faith; Polly learned fast but sometimes the way seemed miry, dark and heavy, and themselves spiritually shrivelled and useless, though they tried to put at God's service the civic influence of a senior place in the Customs.

They made their home a centre of hospitality and joy, though Newton rather restrained his sallies of wit and the turning of impromptu rhymes because the applause of the company fed his vanity. Like all evangelicals of the day they banished dancing, cards and theatre-going, and thus were called Methodists, enthusiasts, and mad; then he picked up a book by John Wesley on broken oaths, which condemned the almost universal habit among officials of accepting bribes or inducements which they had sworn, on entering office, to refuse. Newton thereupon stopped taking gratuities from captains and owners. The Collector of Customs laughed at this new scruple, saying such perquisities were allowed for, and the oath a mere form of words. The polite world of Liverpool rated Newton all the more mad, and the considerable loss of income embarrassed him for a while, especially as the Newtons loved to relieve the poor.

Liverpool considered him equally odd when their Tide Surveyor went into print and sent to the local clergy and dissenting ministers a short paper entitled *Thoughts on Religious Associations*, suggesting ways of improving the religious life of the town. He wrote for a civic society another paper on the subject which was better received and distributed widely by its officials: thus Newton was becoming well known – or notorious – to his fellow townsmen.

In August 1756, a year after Newton joined the Customs and Excise, the Seven Years War broke out. Hostilities at sea reduced the flow of commerce and thus the work of a tide surveyor. Newton used his generous leave to take Polly into Yorkshire, where the evangelical revival had spread in marked contrast to Liverpool. In particular he developed admiration and affection for one of the most unusual characters of the early revival, William Grimshaw, parson of Haworth, the isolated parish on the fells which became even more celebrated in the next century as the home of the Brontes.

Grimshaw had tamed a wild crew in a wild country. The people were more afraid of the parson than of a justice; his reproof was so stern, yet so mild and friendly, that the stoutest sinner could not stand before him and the people loved him. Crowds from far and near thronged his church, yet he often cheerfully walked miles in winter, in storms of wind, rain or snow, upon lonely unsheltered moors, to preach to small companies of aged decrepit people in cottages.

Grimshaw's sense of the evil of sin, of the worth of souls, and the nearness of eternity, fired Newton's heart, and Polly's. And Grimshaw's quarter-deck manner helped awaken in Newton a slumbering hope that one day he too might be captain of a parish or pastorate. He had never forgotten his mother's wish. He meditated on the Apostle

142

Paul's words about the early disciples: 'They heard that he which persecuted us in times past, now preacheth the faith which he once destroyed. And they glorified God in me . . .' Newton saw these words as peculiarly apt for himself and longed for a similar public opportunity. He reckoned that he was more fit than most to be set forth, like Paul, as an example of sinners whom Christ Jesus came into the world to save, and that he had obtained mercy for that purpose.

However, Newton had been too often tongue-tied, both privately, as at Chatham one day when he had tried to say something about Christ to Polly's mother at tea; and publicly, as when he had gone to a meeting in Spitalfields where people might testify. He had silently criticized the style and delivery of those who spoke before him yet when he stood up himself he did much worse. And as with many future clergy his first attempt from a pulpit was a disaster; by 1756 he had concluded that God had not called him to the honour and privilege of being a preacher of the amazing grace of God.

But in Yorkshire he was frequently asked to tell his story, at Haworth and its hamlets and wherever he travelled, among churchmen and dissenters alike. He began to lose his shyness in public. He told his tale so artlessly, with many a whimsical touch and graphic scene, that the people hung on his words. Each visit made him a more acceptable speaker, especially as he passed from mere autobiography, however dramatic, to exposition of the gospel behind the conversion, until early in 1758 some of his Yorkshire friends startled him by proposing that he take holy orders.

He had continued to educate himself despite concluding that he was too tongue-tied to be a minister. He mastered the Greek of the New Testament and the Septuagint; he read the best writers in divinity he could lay hands on in English and Latin, and some in French, for he had picked up French in his seafaring. He had just begun to teach himself Hebrew, a massive task for a mariner whose formal

143

education had stopped at his eleventh birthday; he found it dry and tedious to learn.

When the Yorkshiremen proposed ordination Newton resolved to make Hebrew a test: he would not consider the question until he could read a chapter in the Hebrew Bible with tolerable ease.

By the end of June he could read the historical books and Psalms, although the prophets drove him to lexicons. He therefore bought a notebook in which to jot down over the next few weeks his thoughts on the great proposal. His thirty-third birthday fell on 4 August 1758 (by the New Style calendar. Since 1752 Newton had accepted the logic of the 'lost Eleven Days' and kept 4 August instead of 24 July, just as 'the Fourth of June' became famous as the birthday of George III, born 24 May 1739 when Britain still observed the Julian calendar.) Newton set 4 August apart to close all deliberations on whether to offer for the Christian ministry. From six in the morning he fasted and prayed. Around five in the evening he reached assurance. He would be ordained. From that time on he waited only for clear direction as to where and when; inwardly he regarded himself as already 'torn from the world and worldly concerns and appointed for sanctuary service'.

He rather assumed that his vocation would lie with the Independent Dissenters among whom his mother had brought him up – the people of Dr. Jennings and Samuel Brewer and the late Isaac Watts. But a romantic episode, quite in keeping with the extraordinary twists of his story, changed his direction.

A girl named Kitty, a close friend of the Newtons in Liverpool, had been bereaved of her brother, a Christian like herself, who had died young. Kitty was in love with a rich young man of Hunslet in Yorkshire. Her father forbade the match because the suitor was a 'Methodist', but on the first anniversary of his son's death he relented and begged Newton to escort her to the wedding which he refused to attend himself. Newton left for Hunslet in a hurry, without his boots or his superior's leave, and duly delivered the bride.

While staying at Hunslet vicarage for Kitty's wedding he had much talk with his host, Harry Crook, a friend of Wesley and of Whitefield. Crook not only overcame Newton's scruples about the Church of England but offered a title to holy orders as his curate. Newton returned to Liverpool to consult Polly.

His stipend would be a quarter of his present earnings. After thought and prayer, and Polly's cheerful acceptance of the sacrifices, he wrote accepting. He told Harry Crook that all religious persuasions had their faults and that the Established Church was the best route to reach the people, most of whom were ignorant of the great truths of the gospel.

Newton now needed character testimonials from three clergymen. The first three he approached in Liverpool refused to give them to 'a man who mixed with Methodists'. He found others and in December 1758 left Polly for Leeds, received his title from Crook and took coach to London where he should find the bishop of his own diocese, Chester, attending the House of Lords. He sought hospitality with a family where, to mutual surprise, he met Polly's father. Old Mr. Catlett had heard of his son-in-law turning preacher and was grieved, because he thought it must be among the Independents; both of them were uneasy all evening while in company, but once they were alone and John could explain, Catlett brightened and offered a Rochester acquaintance, Dr. Soan, rector of three livings and headmaster of the grammar school, who was said to be seeking a curate and could pay more than Crook.

Then came utter disappointment. The Bishop of Chester, the rich and proud Dr. Keene, who by law might ordain one of his own flock if he wished, refused to do more than countersign the testimonials. He sent Newton to the Archbishop of York, Mr. Crook's diocesan, the elderly, idle Dr. Gilbert, who was also in London.

The Archbishop declined to receive John Newton, let alone ordain him. 'His Grace,' said the secretary in softest tones, 'was inflexible in supporting the rules and canons of the church' – and one rule, broken by no means rarely, was that a man could not be admitted to holy orders unless holding a degree from Oxford or Cambridge.

The absurdity of this excuse by the Archbishop was well put by John Wesley after he dined with the Newtons in Liverpool some little while later. Wesley knew that the standards for an Oxford or Cambridge degree were then notoriously low, and he wrote in the next volume of his published journal: 'I had a good deal of conversation with Mr. N – – – –n. His case is very peculiar: our Church requires that clergymen should be men of learning, and to this end have a university education: but how many have a university education and yet no learning at all: Yet these men are ordained! Meantime one of eminent learning as well as unblameable behaviour, cannot be ordained, "because he was not at the university"! What a mere farce is this? Who would believe that any Christian Bishop would stoop to so poor an evasion?'

Newton did not doubt that the real reason was his fervent evangelical message and activity. He was suspected of Enthusiasm and rejected as an improper if not a dangerous person, charged with designing to create a disturbance in the Church, 'though it would have been my aim to unite rather than divide'.

Nevertheless he felt humiliated, especially after he had pursued the matter right up to the Archbishop of Canterbury. In Liverpool much excitement had been caused by the Tide Surveyor leaving to become a curate; and the further news that he had been refused holy orders provoked such resounding gossip that Newton could scarcely see three people talking in a street but he assumed they discussed him.

A Yorkshire Independent offered ordination. Newton declined. Wesley offered to make him one of his itinerant lay preachers, but a constitution broken by Africa would not have stood thirty mile rides in the rain; moreover the pittance and the absences would put Polly in want and loneliness. And he disliked the sourness and gloominess of some of Wesley's preachers, though he loved 'the people called Methodist'. He continued as Tide Surveyor. One day he escaped with his life when some business on shore detained him until he reached the boat late, to his vexation and the surprise of the crew, who knew of his strict punctuality at all times. They rowed him out to inspect a ship. As they neared her she blew up with loss of all hands; a few minutes earlier and he would have died with them.

Customs business grew so slack at the height of the war that the Collector gave Newton three months' leave in 1760 to accept temporary charge of an Independent meeting house at Cow Lane in Warwick. He left Polly at Chatham for a short visit, heard Whitefield preach in London, breakfasted with him and found him delighted that Newton wanted to engage 'in the good work' some way or other. He boarded the stage coach for Warwick and went back along the Liverpool road which Polly and he had travelled by chaise a few days earlier. Even early nineteenth-century travellers, in the heyday of stage coaches after the Telford and Macadam improvements, had little idea how tedious were the rough, steep, twisting, main roads which Newton, the Wesleys and Whitefield endured, not least in the Home Counties around London. The quite adventurous journey to Warwick emphasized his loneliness. He would recall how at this bank his dear Polly got off to walk down the hill, at this gate she mounted again—here she laughed, here she cried, 'Oh dear, I shall be down!' He found he was like a

147

child in all concerning her, missing her more than on an African voyage.

At Warwick he settled to his little charge with great expectations. 'Fear not, Paul,' he read as he wandered in the open fields at his devotions, 'I have much people in this city;' this promise in Acts of the Apostles must be claimed as his own. But he soon discovered, as he put it quaintly, 'that Paul was not John and Corinth was not Warwick!' Nevertheless at the end of the three months the congregation urged him to resign from the Customs and become their permanent minister.

The Newtons were undecided. John returned to Liverpool while Polly used the opportunity for another visit to her parents, and he wrote to her 'in a good deal of anxiety and suspense about our Warwick affair, and I have nowhere to unburden myself, or if I had a thousand friends, they would signify little without you.' Her brother Jack, a rising lawyer in London, urged him angrily not to become a despised and impecunious dissenting minister: John's religion, he said, made him behave with the madness of a man blinded by passion; he should consider whether vanity and pride were not the real motives.

John and Polly after much deliberation and prayer sent the Warwick Dissenters a refusal. Church of England orders would have incomparably wider influence in a land where that Church alone was Established by law and held the allegiance of the bulk of the people. 'As to laying aside all thoughts of the ministry,' Newton wrote to Captain Clunie in the summer of 1762, 'it is quite out of my power. I cannot, I will not give up the desire, though I hope I shall not "run before I am sent".'

Yet he nearly did so. Yorkshire friends urged him to open an Independents (Dissenting) Chapel of his own in Liverpool, where he already held small informal services in the Edmund Street house on Sunday evenings with plenty of hymn singing. Sick of hiding his light under a bushel as a layman, he leant strongly towards this idea, with Yorkshire help promised for the first months. But Polly knew better. She saw it as a rash step which he would soon regret. She employed all her love and womanly arts to stop him. He remained adamant. She persevered. And she won. Thirty years afterwards he admitted that no arguments but hers could have dissuaded him. She 'kept me quiet until the Lord's time came when I should have the desire of my heart. The Lord's time is like the time of the tide, which no human power can either accelerate or retard. Though it tarry, wait for it.'

As a sea captain Newton knew how imperceptible is the actual turn of the tide. During a visit to Oxford he met a young Cornishman, a curate named Thomas Haweis. Soon afterwards the curate lost his episcopal licence for being too evangelical and moved to London. They corresponded. By his letters Haweis became the friend Newton lacked in Liverpool – a man of intellect and spirit to whom he could open his heart, his doubts and difficulties. Haweis directed his studies in Hebrew, Greek and church history.

It happened that at the end of 1762 Haweis was staying at Sandwich on the Kentish coast and met another friend of Newton's, a Dissenting minister named Fawcett, who showed him letters which Newton had written the previous summer with some description of his adventures and miseries in Africa, and of the way in which amazing grace had saved 'a wretch like me'. Intrigued, Haweis wrote at once for a fuller account. In January 1763 Newton replied with the first of fourteen letters each filling both sides of a quarto sheet written close, and written in haste as letters between friends, with no thought of publication. Haweis took them to the Earl of Dartmouth, the rich young nobleman who a few years before, through the friendship of the Countess of Huntingdon, had become an ardent Christian. He was almost the only evangelical peer and already a man of influence; later he was George III's Secretary of State for

149

the colonies at the outbreak of the American revolution. By Haweis' action Lord Dartmouth came to know John Newton's story, his qualities, and his desire to be a clergyman.

One year later, in January 1764, Newton consulted Haweis concerning ordination to a Presbyterian church in Yorkshire; despairing of holy orders in the Church of England Newton had decided to accept but the elders set awkward conditions on which he needed advice. At that very moment Lord Dartmouth offered Haweis the parish of Olney in Buckinghamshire, a living in his gift. It would be a curacy to an absentee incumbent; the curate would be entirely his own master though with smaller stipend.

Haweis needed a living himself, yet urged Dartmouth to offer this curacy to Newton, and told Newton what he had done. Newton did not hesitate a moment between a parish and a Presbyterian chapel. On 26 February 1764 he wrote accepting Olney. Once again Newton's life story had turned on the narrowest coincidence. Had the proposal been deferred one week longer it would have been too late: he would have become a Presbyterian.

On 4 March, in the parlour in Edmund Street, Newton broke open a seal carrying the Earl of Dartmouth's arms and read the official offer of Olney in his own hand. Within it lay a note from Haweis urging him to drop everything and come to London at once for ordination. Polly was not afraid to stay by herself and their maids in Liverpool, for she was overjoyed that her John would not be buried away as a Dissenting pastor in Yorkshire.

Arrived in London Newton stayed with Haweis and went with him on the Sunday to the chapel near Hyde Park Corner where he assisted. After the service Lord Dartmouth came round to the pew where Newton sat and carried him off to dinner. Events appeared to move fast. The Bishop of Lincoln, in whose diocese Olney lay, sent word to Lord Dartmouth that the new Archbishop of York would be holding a private ordination next day: if Newton wished to be among those to be ordained he must at once be examined by the Archbishop's chaplain.

Newton received the note an hour after he should have been there, and ran almost the whole way, nearly a mile and a half – only to be kept waiting two hours, and then to suffer a bitter shock. The Archbishop's secretary hummed and hawed and at length said, 'Sir, not to mince the matter, you know you were formerly disappointed. His Grace has heard of it and desires to be excused.' The Bishop of Lincoln could do as he pleased.

Newton, disconcerted, ran back to St. James's Square, arriving in time not to interrupt Lord Dartmouth's dinner, and returned to the Archbishop, whose political interests would lean him towards doing Dartmouth a favour, with a letter from the Earl which opened the way to the Archbishop himself. Archbishop Hay Drummond was a warm-hearted, rather convivial prelate, and though he still made his excuses he was sure the Bishop of Lincoln would ordain. But Newton, hungry and weary, feared York's refusal would stop the whole affair; and it gave Thomas Haweis such a fit of the vapours that he could hardly eat his supper or speak another word that evening. Newton described all these happenings in great detail to Polly.

Lord Dartmouth paid a call on him next day, an act of condescension from a great magnate to a mere tide surveyor which showed Christian humility and love. He brought encouragement from the Bishop of Lincoln. Newton was not wholly free from anxiety, but the Bishop, though he had gone into print against Whitefield, treated Newton with honesty and gentleness, discussed at length his few remaining scruples about the Church, and promised to ordain him.

On 29 April 1764, in the Chapel of the Bishop of Lincoln's great palace at Buckden near Huntingdon, John Newton became a Clerk in Holy Orders of the Church of England. He wrote to Polly: 'Oh what zeal, faith, patience, watchfulness and courage will be needful for my support and guidance! My only hope is in the name and power of Jesus. May that precious name be as ointment poured forth to your soul and mine. May that power be triumphantly manifested in our weakness!'

He rode across country (could it be then that *How Sweet the Name* took shape?) for a peep at Olney and its people. He returned to Liverpool to settle his affairs and collect Polly. And Liverpool, which had despised and objected to its evangelistic tide surveyor, turned round and gave him a great send-off by inviting him to preach in the parish church before the mayor and corporation.

As he looked at the great congregation of friends and neighbours high and low his heart was overwhelmed with praise to God 'for putting me into the ministry. No one could be more *unworthy*, for I had been long a persecutor and blasphemer and a profligate. And considering my situation, connections and habits of life, no one could be more *unlikely*!'

18

The Music of Thy Name

Above the fireplace of his study in Olney vicarage John
Newton put an inscription, painted in clear letters so that
he could not ignore it whenever he entered the room.

Formed from two texts of Scripture, one from Isaiah, the
other from Deuteronomy, it read:

> *Since thou wast precious in my sight thou hast been honourable.*
> *But thou shalt remember that thou wast a bondman in Egypt,*
> *and the Lord thy God redeemed thee.*

Through forty-three years of ordained ministry Newton
always did remember. 'Never,' he wrote, 'was there a more
clearly demonstrated proof of the freeness and efficacy of
divine grace – powerful to change the most hardened
offender, and merciful to forgive the most aggravated
offences.'

The present book is the story of that 'amazing grace'
rather than a full biography of Newton, but some description
of his ministry in Olney, and later in London, must round
it off.

John and Polly Newton took up residence in their parish
on 26 May 1764. Olney was then a small market town with
one long main street beside a stream, which so frequently
flooded that the folk had built a raised causeway in the
centre of the road. At the south end of the town flowed the
Ouse, which also overflowed its banks. The coach road

crossed the river and water meadows by a long bridge of irregular arches. The immediate countryside was flat and dreary with frequent mists and fogs. Olney men worked the fields and the women pored for ten or twelve hours a day making pillow lace in their thatched cottages, where the confined air tended to give them lung trouble and sometimes affected their minds. Most of the inhabitants lived from hand to mouth. Newton's heart stretched out to them, and when, almost immediately, he received through a friend of Polly's father the offer of a more lucrative living near London, he refused it.

In addition to Sunday services he had already started a less formal weeknight 'lecture' in the old church with its tower topped by a spire. Each Thursday he borrowed a room in Lord Dartmouth's disused Great House, an old manor fallen into a neglected and rather filthy state, for a children's meeting, an innovation which anticipated Robert Raikes' famous Sunday school movement by fifteen years. Eighty-nine children came the first time, almost more than the room could contain, and his aim was to 'talk, preach, and reason with them, and explain the Scriptures to them in their own little way'. He taught them plenty of hymns; he shrewdly instituted a system of rewards for knowledge and good behaviour; but it was his manner and affection, and not least his sea stories which drew them.

Newton quickly won his parishioners' love. Unlike many rural clergy of the day he visited them frequently in their sickness and their health and regarded himself as their servant. Here was no coldly distant scholar or idle sprig of the gentry but a jolly sea captain turned parson; deeply serious in teaching and aims, something of the quarter-deck about him, but larding his sermons with anecdotes and nautical allusions, and his conversation with quaint sayings and touches of fun. He seldom wore clerical dress on weekdays, preferring to visit in his old sea jacket, whereas neighbouring clergy wore clerical dress when riding to hounds or shooting with their squires.

The people flocked to hear him. 'Neither short days, uncertain weather or dirty roads,' he wrote to Alex Clunie that first winter, 'make any considerable diminution in our assemblies, and their attention and seriousness give me hope that they do not all come in vain.' Within a year he had to add a gallery to the church.

He was not a polished preacher. He preached extempore, and did not always prepare as he should. Articulation was poor and gestures ungraceful, yet he held his hearers by the strength and passion of his convictions and the love which shone through his words. He used to say that the point in all his preaching was 'to break a hard heart and to heal a broken heart'. He did not preach too long, aware that an overlong sermon competes in the listener's mind with the pudding overboiling at home, but the sermon formed the centre of the service, always expounding Scripture.

Newton did not overrate his early success, built as it was on a foundation laid by his predecessor; and if ever he felt proud he would take a dash of 'Plantain sauce' by recalling his African days of sin and starvation. Not that Olney brought wealth. He had been earning much more at Liverpool; the expenses of moving and settling ate into reserves; and within a few months his small savings disappeared when Manesty the ship-owner went bankrupt, ruined by the strangulation of trade in the Seven Years' War, and soon afterwards died.

But, 'When one spring dries up, the Lord opens another.' Thomas Haweis and Alex Clunie, who now held a post in the Customs and Excise in London, had persuaded Newton to publish the letters in which he had told the extraordinary story of his adventures and conversion. Haweis provided a preface, Clunie arranged the printing, and in August 1764 an immediate bestseller appeared, at first anonymously: *An Authentic Narrative of Some Remarkable and Interesting Particulars in the Life of* ***, *communicated, in a Series of Letters, to the Rev. T. Haweis*. The sums due to the author arrived at a critical time, especially as the Newtons dipped into their pockets to relieve parish distress.

An Authentic Narrative reached all classes. At Olney, little groups would gather in the cottages and a 'scholard' would read it aloud to illiterate neighbours. Everybody knew the letters had been written by their parson. 'The people stare at me,' Newton told Clunie, 'and well they may. I am indeed a wonder to many, a wonder to myself; especially I wonder that I wonder no more.' In cold print, the grace that saved him looked even more amazing, yet he had not given half the detail of 'my wickedness, misery and hair-breadth escapes as my memory would have furnished'.

Newton quickly recognized that his book placed the marvel of God's grace before many who would not listen to Whitefield or Wesley. It brought correspondence and visits from seekers and learners in the faith. It strengthened friendships. One in particular did good to Olney. Newton had already met the richest merchant in England, John Thornton, who was Whitefield's convert and Lord Dartmouth's friend. After reading *An Authentic Narrative* and visiting Olney Thornton asked Newton to accept an annual sum of two hundred pounds: 'Be hospitable and keep an open house . . . Help the poor and needy,' and draw on him for more whenever there was occasion. Newton reckoned that when he left Olney after fifteen years the then very considerable sum of three thousand pounds had passed through his hands from Thornton.

An Authentic Narrative played a part in bringing to Olney the man whose name will always be associated with Newton's: William Cowper, then aged thirty-two and not yet the most celebrated poet of his age.

The frail, nervous Cowper had already recovered from two periods of insanity and three attempts at suicide. His family had placed him in the care of a kindly physician of

St. Albans, Nathaniel Cotton. In the same summer, 1764, that the Newtons went to Olney, William Cowper recovered his sanity after coming into evangelical faith through the influence of his cousin, Martin Madan (to whom Thomas Haweis had been curate) and Cotton's gentle teaching and care.

In the summer of 1767 Cowper was living as 'a sort of adopted son' with a clerical family, Morley and Mary Unwin, at Huntingdon, the county town close to the bishop's palace where Newton had been ordained deacon and priest. The Unwins showed Cowper Newton's book. After reading it he wrote a manuscript of his own conversion for strictly private circulation, and was therefore delighted when he heard that a mutual friend had suggested the Newtons visit the Unwins to meet Cowper, on their way home from a tour among old acquaintance in Lancashire and Yorkshire.

The Newtons arrived in July to find a stricken household: Morley Unwin had been killed by a fall from his horse three days before. The widow, with her unmarried daughter and Cowper, wished to leave Huntingdon as soon as possible and asked Newton among others to look around. By 18 July Cowper was writing to his aunt, Mrs. Madan: 'Mr. Newton seems to have conceived a great desire to have us for neighbours, and I am sure we shall think ourselves highly favoured to be committed to the care of such a pastor.' In August they visited Olney and settled on a house of somewhat severe appearance and bad repair on the south side of the market place, called Orchard Side. While it was being made ready they stayed with the Newtons for nearly five months.

Newton and Cowper became close friends at once. Besides a common faith they shared a love of poetry and of the countryside and were hard walkers. Both of them had a great sense of humour, though Cowper's melancholy was never far away. He was an enthusiastic gardener and so was Polly, doting on their gardens, which were separated by a single field; the two households paid the owner for a right of way to allow them to visit each other's homes and gardens without going round by road. The townsfolk called their new neighbour 'Sir Cowper' or Squire Cowper, for he was cousin to an earl. He loved to visit the poor and sit with the children at the Great House and to walk through rain or snow to the prayer meeting at Molly Mole's cottage, which Newton jocularly dubbed the Mole hill.

While Cowper was still a guest under the Newton's roof, before daybreak on 9 December 1767, when reading the passage in Genesis, 'Enoch walked with God,' he began to compose one of his loveliest hymns, *Oh for a closer walk with God, A calm and Heavenly frame*. After two lines he fell asleep. 'When I awaked again the third and fourth were whispered to my heart in a way which I have often experienced.' He wrote down:

A Light to shine upon the Road
That leads me to the Lamb!

The entire hymn of six verses followed.

He probably read it out at the breakfast table. Within a few months he had written *Hark my Soul! It is the Lord*. Soon Cowper and Newton were stimulating each other to hymn-writing. Together they made Olney famous for its hymns, sending them anonymously to magazines or collections, but later conceiving the plan of producing their own hymnbook.

In the cold spring of 1769 Newton secured Dartmouth's permission to transfer the parish prayer meeting to the Great House's 'great room', which he described as 'a noble place with a parlour behind it, and holds one hundred and thirty people conveniently'; the prayer meeting had outgrown Molly Mole's cottage. The great room needed cleaning and refurbishing. For the formal opening Cowper and Newton each wrote a hymn. Newton wrote *O Lord! our languid souls inspire*, but it is Cowper's *Jesus, where'er Thy people meet* which has become part of earth's Christian heritage. After this Newton, though composition did not come easily, usually turned out one hymn a week to expound and teach at the Great House, and others for the lacemakers to sing in the 'Lace Tellings'. To sing hymns in the parish church itself, except for metrical psalms, still seemed a little daring.

Cowper had written *There is a fountain filled with blood* by 1772, but the actual date of Newton's *How Sweet the Name of Jesus sounds* remains obscure. In the later part of 1772 tragedy struck the partnership. 'Sir Cowper' showed signs of renewed mental derangement, fearing once again that he was eternally damned. Attacks grew more frequent, until madness struck him down early on Sunday 24 January 1773. The Newtons were sent for in haste at four in the morning. Newton stayed until eight, when Cowper seemed calmer, and Polly stayed at his side all day. But Cowper, as he wrote long after, had 'plunged into a melancholy that made me almost an infant'.

The myth that the supposed severity of Newton's ministrations or theology were primarily responsible cannot stand up to the evidence. The Newtons worked hard to save their friend's mind from fear of damnation, to make him laugh at quaint sayings or comic verses or funny stories, to help him feel loved: they even put up with Cowper and Mrs Unwin as uninvited guests for more than a year in the vicarage because he felt happier than in his own Orchard Side.

By October 1773 Cowper seemed more stable, though never smiling or writing or making intelligent conversation, and the Newtons therefore ventured on their annual preaching visit to Warwick and on to Northampton. Here they received an agitated letter from Mrs. Unwin imploring their return: Cowper, convinced that God demanded a human sacrifice, had tried to hang himself. They hurried back. Newton still did not lose 'hope for a happy issue'. It is said, though without firm evidence, that after this suicide attempt Cowper wrote one of the best known of all his hymns, *God moves in a mysterious way*, which was published in 1774.

Cowper's mental illness dried up Newton's hymnwriting.

'My grief and disappointment were great; I hung my harp upon the willows, and for some time thought myself determined to proceed no farther without him.'

At length in April 1774 Cowper smiled again at a little joke. In May he and Mrs. Unwin left the vicarage. His recovery proceeded rapidly, though he never lost a sense of despair, of banishment from God's presence. Newton began to write hymns again, adding another almost weekly. Cowper wrote no more, though his greatest poetry lay ahead.

In 1779 Newton published *Olney Hymns*, 348 pieces by two authors, of which 282 were by Newton. Many of these hardly survived their own day or were too autobiographical for wide acceptance but two or three dozen achieved lasting fame.

Thus the ex-slave trader and ex-sea captain, the one-time blasphemer and writer of scurrilous rhymes, enriched the world's worship by hymns that will never die, sung in countless translations as well as in their original English; hymns such as *How Sweet the name of Jesus sounds*, *Glorious things of thee are spoken*, *May the Grace of Christ our Saviour*, *Be still my heart! these anxious cares*. And *Amazing Grace*.

19

'A Little Odd-looking Man'

'At the archdeacon's visitation at Long Stratford appeared as minister of Olney one Mr. Newton, a little odd-looking man of the methodistical order, and without any clerical habit. He said he was Mr. Browne's curate.' So wrote William Cole, rector of Bletchley, whom posterity celebrates as antiquary rather than as parson. Newton may have been twisting the lion's tail unnecessarily in attending the archdeacon's visitation in his sea jacket but Cole's tone reflects the distaste of neighbouring clergy for Newton as an 'enthusiast'.

He annoyed them further by loving Dissenters, a side of him which did not quite please Polly, always the church-woman. When the local association of Baptist ministers met at Olney in 1768 he attended their meetings and they his lecture in the parish church. Newton was ahead of his time in this, and stood for peace in an age of theological wrangles, even within the evangelical camp. 'I am sick of the spirit of party of all parties,' he once wrote from Olney. 'I wish to be able to throw some water upon the fire of contention. I feel desire of publishing two small pamphlets – one upon the comparative insignificance of forms and modes of worship – the other to show the wrong principles and bad effects of the dispute between the Calvinists and Arminians.'

His closest ministerial friend in the neighbourhood was an Independent named William Bull, who had begun at the next town up river, Newport Pagnell, a few months after

Newton's arrival. A man of intelligence, imagination and wide reading, and a great talker, Bull was then aged twenty-six but it was not for some seven years that the two became warmly attached. Newton found Bull to be Christlike and a deep thinker; Polly liked him and he would come to dinner and to preach at their prayer meetings, the parish church being barred by law to a Dissenter. 'We only want to hear those who can tell us about Jesus and stir us up to live to Him,' he wrote to Bull, and at another time: 'When you are with the King, and getting good for yourself, speak a word for me and mine. I have reason to think you see Him oftener and have nearer access to Him than myself. . . .'

One day they were in Bull's booklined library puffing at their long 'churchwarden' pipes, discussing Scripture as they often did, when a Dissenting minister from Northampton knocked to tell them that the author of *Rock of Ages*, Augustus Toplady, was resting at the Swan: 'He is on his way to London and will not live long.' They hastened to the inn and found an emaciated, disease-stricken clergyman, alert enough to talk. They were interrupted, however, by a noise in the street and were disgusted to see a bull-baiting pass by. Mr. Toplady, distressed at the cruelty to the bull, pronounced the sight unbearable were it not that all these poor suffering animals would be compensated in heaven.

'I certainly hope that all *bulls* will go to heaven,' punned William Bull, 'but will *all* the animal creation?'

'Yes, certainly,' said Toplady with great emphasis, for this was one of his pet beliefs. 'All, all!'

'What,' exclaimed Newton jokingly, recalling shipboard discomfort, 'Do you suppose, sir, there will be *fleas* in heaven? I have a special aversion to fleas!'

Toplady looked hurt, though he held his peace. But when Newton begged him to stay at Olney should he come that way again, the author of *Rock of Ages* replied quite rudely (for he was a trifle cantankerous even in health) to the author of *How Sweet the Name* who wanted no fleas in heaven.

Newton's nearest clerical neighbour in later years at Olney, the curate of the next village to the west, held him in contempt and derision. This was a young clergyman of rough country background, self-educated, named Thomas Scott. He was more interested in teaching himself Hebrew than in the people of his parish but was ashamed when he learned that Newton had several times visited two dying parishioners of Scott's, a man and wife, whom he had neglected himself because 'not sent for'. He went to their cottage, found one already dead, and with much remorse attempted to do his pastoral duty by the other.

Scott scarcely believed in Christ's divinity. At the next archdeacon's visitation (to stifle his bad conscience about the dead cottagers) he tried angrily to argue the point with Newton, who declined to be drawn. They began a correspondence. Scott attempted to stir up controversy and 'filled my letters with definitions, enquiries, arguments, objections . . . He, on the other hand, shunned everything controversial as much as possible and filled his letters with the most useful and least offensive instructions,' only dropping occasional hints of the necessity of faith and how it could be found. This annoyed Scott and he dropped the correspondence and shunned Newton's company —until a time of discouragement led him to call at Olney vicarage, where he found help.

Mutual affection grew; Scott attended Newton's weekday lectures; at length, nearly four years after the incident of the cottagers, Scott 'began to perceive our Lord's meaning when he says, "Except ye receive the kingdom of heaven as a little child, ye shall in no wise enter therein." ' Scott's story of his conversion, *The Force of Truth*, is a classic of spiritual autobiography. A monumental biblical commentary and many other books made him in after years one of the most influential evangelicals of his day.

Newton was already influential by his books, far beyond Olney. Long ago he had begun an Ecclesiastical History 'to trace the gospel spirit, its abuses and the oppositions to it, through the several ages of the Church', and worked at it off and on for years. It had got no further than the close of the Acts of the Apostles when published in 1770, but Joseph Milner of Hull took up the theme and gave the world his celebrated history. Newton had expected to do most good in print by literary works but from *An Authentic Narrative* onwards it was the publication of letters which made him well known, 'letters which I wrote without study, or any public design. But the Lord said, "You shall be most useful by *them*," and I learned to say, "Thy will be done! Use me as thou pleasest, only *make* me useful." '

Letter writing became one of his chief ministries; by the end of his life he had written thousands in his neat, small handwriting, to scores of correspondents. His habit was to write once a quarter ('my quarterly budget') to his friends and his disciples, unless some anniversary or occasion or problem required more frequent communication. Since his circle enlarged continually, and he was unstinting in replies to strangers, he spent hours every week at his desk. He wrote from the heart and the letters reached the heart, for his own past and his learning, and his experience with souls, gave him profound insight into what he called 'the study of the human heart, with its workings and counterworkings, as it is differently affected in a state of nature and of grace.' Whenever he borrowed back a few and published them the books became favourites with the public, especially *Cardiphonia*, the 'sound of the heart', a title suggested by Cowper. *Cardiphonia* was soon republished in America and translated into French and Dutch.

Newton's private or published letters brought a stream of guests to Olney vicarage, a cheerful house with plenty of laughter and welcome. Since the Newtons had no children yet were fond of them they gladly adopted Polly's orphaned nieces Betsy Catlett and Elizabeth Cunningham; Eliza died in childhood after showing a beautiful faith and character which Newton described feelingly in a pamphlet The household always stayed united, with master and mistress treating their maids, Sally and Molly, almost as members of the family; Newton made a point of friendship with servants, and often wrote quaint letters of simple spiritual advice to the servants of houses where he had stayed.

As their own guests could not fail to realize, Newton and Polly remained much in love. When she was away looking after her aged father they wrote frequent letters, his flowing with ideas and encouragements, hers brief and stilted but none the less deep; and, as she once put it, 'I write sheets in my mind.' His would begin, 'My dearest charming Polly,' or 'My dearest Charmer,' or 'My dearest sweetest, dear Polly, alias Mary'; and hers 'My own precious dear'. They still felt intensely any separation: as Newton wrote to her while staying with Thornton at Clapham, 'I am always a little awkward without you, and every room where you are not present looks unfurnished.' They kept touch by prayer. Almost every hour each would bring the other to the mind's eye and shape prayers according to probable whereabouts and activity. This was easier for Polly because Newton regulated his Olney days by shipboard precision.

Polly had been a somewhat nervous creature ever since the shock of his sudden collapse at Liverpool in '55. She would be thrown into agitation if she thought her absent John in trouble or danger, as during the great blizzard of January 1776 when he had planned to join her in London, to bring her back with her father. He begged her 'not to give way to fears on my account, or to calculate the depth of the snow at present or of the floods when the snow shall melt. Since you have had an interest in me the Lord has preserved me from innumerable dangers of which you could form no idea. We may safely trust Him. His arm is not weary nor is He at any time afar off. He is always near and providence always watches over them that fear Him. But I know I cannot reason you out of your apprehensions — therefore I would turn my thoughts upwards and say, Lord do Thou keep her heart stayed upon Thee, and maintain Thy peace in her, and give her a power of trusting all in Thy hand and submitting all to Thy will.'

On the other hand a delayed letter from Polly meant agitation for John, but joy when the stage coach brought it. 'I waited about the street yesterday,' he wrote from Olney, 'until it was time to go to Orchard Side, and then deputed Molly to supply my place. At half-past four the horn sounded and my heart went pit-a-pat. But I soon saw Molly pass the window, and by her looks and speed I guessed she had a letter. I snatched it from her and read it, and was presently well.'

Newton had intended to remain at Olney until he died. He had refused a country living, with its increased stipend and status, which was in the gift of Thornton. He had been tempted when he thought he might be offered Halifax, a rising industrial town in Yorkshire, but glad when he was not. Later he refused Lord Dartmouth's offer of the presidency of the college in Savannah, Georgia, which Whitefield, now dead, had founded. Yet towards the end of the 1770s his ministry in Olney was losing momentum. It was not because Newton, like Grimshaw who had ruled Haworth with an iron rod, tried too hard to discipline the parish. He could be fierce when he chose, as on the day when local lads hooted at a funeral procession; but the trouble lay quite the other way. He made himself too cheap and he lacked discrimination. William Bull put it well, in Cowper's hearing, some two years after Newton had left Olney. 'Mr. Newton,' said Bull, 'trod a path which no man but himself could have used so long as he did, and he wore it out long before he went from Olney. Too much familiarity and condescension cost him the estimation of his people. He thought he should insure their love, to which he had the best possible title, and by those very means he lost it.'

They no longer listened as of old. A hard core of

incorrigibles resisted the gospel. Divisions sprang up between those who attended the parish church on Sundays only and those who came also to the lectures and the Great House. The local clergy, by now, accepted him as a benevolent and industrious minister even when they deplored his evangelical doctrines, and the whole neighbourhood loved him for his help to the sufferers when a dreadful fire destroyed part of Olney in October 1777; yet this very disaster led to an incident which shook Newton profoundly.

Since most of the town dwellings were thatched, Newton sensibly suggested after the fire that the inhabitants should forego their customary riotous, drunken bonfire orgy on 5 November, Guy Fawkes Day, when with all England they celebrated the national deliverance long ago from gunpowder, treason and plot. The celebration committee agreed and asked him to give notice in church. 'I really understood it to be the general sense of the town.'

On the evening of 5 November 1777 a 'wild and lawless mob', enraged by the prohibition, paraded down the long street breaking windows and demanding money with menaces. A cottager rushed to warn the Newtons that the rioters were yelling that they were on the way to the vicarage to smash every window. Polly's nerve gave way. Terrified, with a knocking growing louder inside her head, she clung to John.

The queller of mutineers prepared to face the rioters. He believed that singly they could have been reasoned with, 'but in a body, and when influenced with drink, they are terrible creatures', yet no worse than violent slaves determined to regain liberty.

At ten o'clock that night a friend hammered on the door. He warned Newton that forty or fifty, 'full of fury and liquor' were about to assault the house: their yelling could be heard through the closed windows. Polly could stand it no longer. She implored John to bribe them to go away.

As he told Thornton, 'I was forced to send an embassy and beg peace. A soft message, and a shilling to the captain of the mob, secured his protection and we slept in safety. 'Alas, "tell it not in Gath!" I am ashamed of the story.'

20

Killing the Slave Trade

In the city of London, in Lombard Street which was famous for its wealthy bankers, stood an unusual, monumental church designed by Hawksmoor: St. Mary Woolnoth. John Thornton had acquired the presentation and when the incumbent died in 1779 he offered the living to Newton.

'London is the last situation I should have chosen for myself,' commented Newton. 'I love woods and fields and streams and trees – to hear the bird sing and the sheep bleat.' But he accepted, recognizing that while usefulness at Olney decreased, Thornton's offer would make him an evangelical incumbent in London; and among all the city churches there was only one other at that decisive time in the affairs of church and state. Another City magnate then disputed the right of presentation, which involved Thornton in litigation and Newton in suspense. He had quipped to Bull: 'I am about to form a connection for life with one Mary Woolnoth, a reputed London saint in Lombard Street.' Now he had to write: 'Molly Woolnoth and I are not yet married. I told you someone forbid the banns, and the prohibition is not yet taken off, but I believe we shall soon hasten *into the midst of things*.' To wed Molly, he said, would be pleasing, but to be divorced from Olney would be painful.

The House of Lords found in Thornton's favour. In December 1779 Newton preached his first sermon at St. Mary Woolnoth, but did not preach his farewell at Olney until January 1780, Polly following him to London in March. Cowper's distress at the loss of the Newtons was well expressed in his remark about the arrival to the pulpit and the vicarage of one Benjamin Page: 'If he is not spotless, his spots will be seen, and the plainer, because he comes after Mr. Newton.' Page soon resigned in favour of Thomas Scott. In the eyes of many, none could replace John Newton: 'You were greatly loved at Olney,' Cowper told him.

Newton, now in his middle fifties, quickly established a unique position in London. A rector or vicar in the eighteenth century had a prestige above any Dissenter, above any Church of England curate, lecturer or minister of a proprietary chapel. The parish of St. Mary Woolnoth was small but important, for it included the Mansion House, so that the Lord Mayor for each year was a parishioner, a matter of awe to Newton: 'That one of the most ignorant, the most miserable and the most abandoned of slaves should be plucked from his forlorn state of exile on the coast of Africa and at length be appointed minister of the parish of the first magistrate of the first city in the world – that he should there not only testify of such grace but stand up as a singular instance and monument of it, is a fact I can contemplate with admiration, but never sufficiently estimate.'

His testifying of grace soon brought a large congregation to his church though he neither expected nor drew the vast audiences which hung on Wesley's lips. One of his best series of sermons was provoked by the Handel Commemoration sung in Westminster Abbey, for though Newton enjoyed Handel he disapproved of Scripture being made into musical entertainment, as he regarded it. To improve the occasion he preached at St. Mary Woolnoth fifty sermons in the course of two years, expounding the Scriptures which form the libretto of Handel's *Messiah*. They were afterwards published. Newton was mildly a Calvinist but in that age of fierce theological disputation he tried to 'keep all shibboleths, and forms and terms of distinction out of sight, as we keep knives and razors out of the way of children, and if my hearers had not other means of information I think they would not know from me that there are such creatures as Arminians and Calvinists in the world. But we talk a good deal about Christ.'

Many of Newton's hearers came from a distance, often after reading one of his books. His influence never ceased to amaze him. He had, he mused, 'longed for an opportunity of preaching the gospel in some remote corner, and looked no farther. Could I expect that God should appoint me in a very public post, give me that liberty and acceptance with which I have been since favoured, and enable me to write, what has made my worthless name known to His people far and near?'

Success never induced pride; he knew his heart. This was beautifully and quaintly described in a letter he had written at Olney when a lion came to the Cherry Fair: 'The lion was wonderfully tame: as familiar with his keeper, as docile and obedient as a spaniel; yet the man told me he had his surly fits, when he durst not touch him. No looking-glass could express my face more justly than this lion did my heart. I could trace every feature. As wild and fierce by nature, yea, much more so; but grace has in some measure tamed me. I know and love my Keeper and sometimes watch His looks that I may learn His will. But oh! I have my surly fits too — seasons when I relapse into the savage again — as though I had forgotten all. I got a hymn out of this lion . . .'

In London the ministry was centred as much on Newton's home as in his church. St. Mary Woolnoth had no rectory. The Newtons lived two miles away in Charles Square, Hoxton, then a pleasant suburb; to their delight they could see green fields and cows, 'so that it has some little resemblance to the country'. They kept open house. The poor would receive relief at the door (the less genuine finding Newton a little too easy a touch) while the afflicted and tempted, after confidential counsel in his study, went away strengthened with sympathy or advice. As a pastor he gave himself unstintingly at home and away. He described his life amusingly to Cowper: 'My time is divided between running about to look on other people, and sitting at home like a tame elephant or a monkey for other people to come and look at me!'

Ministers and lay friends of all denominations, especially young men who were starting or intending a lifetime of Christian service, flocked to his breakfast parties. These began with family prayers. He read a chapter, added a few pithy remarks and then prayed: 'the prayer was never long, but remarkably suitable and simple.'

After breakfast he would take any male guests who were free to remain, and settle to his chair in the study, draw at his long pipe, and puffing away he would converse, recalls William Jay, a Dissenter from Bath, 'in a manner the most easy and free and varied and edifying. There was nothing about him dull or gloomy or puritanical, according to the common meaning of the term. As he had much good nature, so he had much pleasantry, and frequently emitted sparks of lively wit, or rather humour.' Richard Cecil, a fellow clergyman who was afterwards his biographer, said Newton's conversation and habits among friends 'were more peculiar, amusing and instructive than any I ever witnessed.'

Once a fly perched on Newton's nose, making him sneeze. He remarked, 'If this fly keeps a diary, he'll write: "To-day a terrible earthquake!" ' Or he would tell of an old woman whose death bed he attended, who said that despite her guilt and unworthiness she was persuaded that 'my Lord Jesus will save me from all my sins and sorrows and bring me home to Himself. And if He does, *He'll never hear the last of it!*' Jay was with him when Newton received a letter from a man in Bath whom Jay knew to be a scoundrel. 'But,' remarked Newton, 'he writes now like a penitent.'

'If he is,' replied Jay, 'I'll never despair of the conversion of anyone again.'

'Oh,' exclaimed Newton. 'I never did, since God saved me.'

One subject he brought up more and more frequently: the iniquity of the Slave Trade.

'My heart shudders that I was ever engaged in it,' he would say. His awakening had been slow. In 1763–64 when he wrote and published *An Authentic Narrative* he had begun to doubt the moral lawfulness of the Slave Trade he had left ten years earlier but he did not attack it. While he was at Olney, reading widely and in touch with John Wesley, who condemned it in a pamphlet in 1774, he became aware of the growing swell of adverse opinion which made the Trade to stink but as something that could not be abolished without disaster to a nation's economy.

By the time Newton came to London he was appalled by it. He grew intense in his opposition, bewailing this crime against humanity at every opportunity. He became something of an 'Ancient Mariner', buttonholing any who would listen to his stories of the horrors, and his dreadful concern that he should have continued in it when a Christian. He longed to make amends. When the University of New Jersey sent word that they had made him an honorary Doctor of Divinity, he refused to call himself D.D., saying that 'the dreary coast of Africa had been his university and he would never accept any diploma 'except from the poor blacks'.

The Slave Trade would not vanish because an ex-slave trader repented of his past. Only an Act of Parliament could bring in Abolition, and no one could expect a majority in either Commons or Lords to put a stop to the British trade while other nations continued with theirs. In the earlier 1780s Newton could see no prospect of success.

Then one day in December 1785, among the requests received at his vestry for interviews, lay a note signed by a name which made his heart leap: William Wilberforce.

The world knew William Wilberforce as the brilliant, amusing young man of fashion and Member of Parliament who had won Yorkshire for the Prime Minister, William Pitt, his bosom friend and contemporary. Newton knew him as the nephew of his dear friend Hannah Wilberforce, John Thornton's sister. When Wilberforce was eight years old he had lost his father, a rich merchant in Hull, and gone to live with his uncle and aunt in Wimbledon. Newton, up from Olney, had met him there and at Thornton's, and the older Wilberforces had brought him sometimes to Olney. The boy became John Newton's ardent disciple, listening wide eyed to his sea stories, laughing at his jokes, joining in his songs — and coming, as it seemed, to share his faith. Wilberforce revered John Newton almost as a parent. But the boy's mother in Hull became alarmed that he was turning into a little 'methodist'. She removed him from the Wimbledon household and thus from Newton's influence, and weaned him, over the years, from his faith. In 1781, when Wilber-force was twenty-three and already a Member of Parliament, Newton writing to Cowper about another child referred to his lost disciple: 'I am aware religious appearances in so young a subject are to be regarded with caution. The strongest and most promising views of this sort I ever met with were in the case of Mr. Wilberforce when he was a boy — but they seem now entirely worn off, not a trace left behind, except a deportment comparatively decent and moral in a young man of large fortune.'

Four years later in December 1785 Newton received the note at his church begging for a strictly secret interview. Because Wilberforce was an important man, and evangeli-cals were despised and derided by his friends in the world of fashion, he took almost absurd measures to cover his tracks when he went, by appointment, to Newton's house in Charles Square.

Here he unfolded a story of two journeys across France with Isaac Milner, a Yorkshireman who (unknown to Wilberforce) had become an evangelical, and how they had started to read, almost by chance, Philip Doddridge's *Rise and Progress of Religion in the Soul*. This book, and the Bible, had brought him to a spiritual crisis and anguish of soul, for once he had understood the implications of the Christian gospel he could not bring himself to surrender to Christ, fearing loss of position and popularity. By the time he talked to Newton he was willing to yield, indeed had done so, but his naturally joyous personality lay clouded by doubt and dismay and he felt he must confide in a counsellor or go out of his mind. Thus he had turned to his boyhood hero. He told Newton that he wished to resign his seat in Parliament and become a clergyman.

Newton helped him to unburden his conscience; and persuaded him not to disappear into holy orders: God might have raised him up to serve Him in the councils of state, for the good of church and nation.

Wilberforce did not resign from Parliament. By Easter 1786, with the help of Newton and others, he had come to assurance; Newton wrote to Cowper: 'I judge he is now decidedly on the right track . . . I hope the Lord will make him a blessing both as a Christian and a statesman. How seldom do these characters coincide!! But they are not incompatible.'

The old ex-slave trader and the young statesman became firm friends, and whenever they were together Newton used to harp on his shame about the Trade. He was undoubtedly one of the several influences which led Wilberforce to take up Abolition and agree to lay the subject before Parliament.

The details of the long struggle which ended in the Abolition of the Slave Trade twenty one years later belong to Wilberforce's story,* but Newton, until he grew too aged, was in the inner circle of Abolitionists.

And he helped to bring to deep Christian faith in 1787

* See the present writer's *Wilberforce* (Constable, London, 1977; St. Martin's Press, New York, 1978; Lion Paperback, 1978).

one of the most effective among them – Hannah More, the celebrated playwright and wit, renowned as one of the Nine Muses of Great Britain in a famous print. She had several evangelical friends. Contrasting their ways with hers she became dissatisfied in soul and found her way to St. Mary Woolnoth. John Newton showed Hannah More how to place her faith in Christ and her pen at Christ's disposal. Her fame and popularity presented many opportunities in the world of fashion and wealth where she had long moved at ease, and later she devoted herself to the poor of her native West Country and to writings which brought the Christian message to all ranks of British society; and she worked hard with Wilberforce in the cause of Abolition.

When battle was fully joined, Newton produced a devastating pamphlet, as the only Abolitionist leader with first hand experience. 'Silence at such a time,' he wrote in its first pages 'and on such an occasion would, in me, be criminal. If my testimony should not be necessary or serviceable, yet perhaps I am bound in conscience to take shame to myself by a public confession which, however, sincere, comes too late to prevent or repair the misery and mischief to which I have formerly beeen accessory.'

It did not come too late.

Newton was now in his sixty-third year, venerable in appearance and regarded with awe for his past history and present influence. In 1788 the Prime Minister placed the whole subject of the Slave Trade before a committee of the Privy Council with instructions to investigate thoroughly. One of the witnesses summoned by the committee was John Newton. The wheel had come full circle as the ex-slave trader took coach to St. James's Palace.

He mounted the stairs, somewhat painfully because of a bad leg and other aches and pains, and waited in a long corridor beneath portraits of monarchs and princes, until he heard his name called as usher to usher echoed: *The Reverend John Newton!*

176

He walked towards the open door of the committee chamber. As he turned to enter he saw, awaiting him, the Prime Minister himself: Mr. Pitt bowed. The Privy Councillors and all in the room rose to their feet.

The once flogged sailor, the former lecher and blasphemer, the slave trader who had been redeemed from slavery, found himself escorted to his seat by the King's chief minister.

'Oh, Lord, it is all Thy doings, to Thee be also the praise. To me belongs the shame and confusion of face, for I am a poor vile creature to this hour!'

Epilogue

Polly had never fully recovered from the shock of thinking John dead before her eyes in 1754. As the Newtons reached old age, still deeply in love, she suffered nervous or physical disorders with increasing frequency, without losing her cheerful spirit.

Newton's extreme and undisguised attachment used to puzzle some of his friends 'as she seemed to have few or any attractions'. They were obvious enough to him, for she was a dream wife and he had never woken from the dream.

In the autumn of 1788 new pains troubled Polly. She consulted an eminent surgeon. He diagnosed cancer. She begged him to operate when her husband should be away from home so that he would know nothing until it was over, but the surgeon warned her that an operation (without anaesthetics) might be fatal. She did not break the news until the following day that she would probably be the first to die, within two years at most. A shocked Newton tried to face the prospect in submission to the will of God, but 'strongly felt I was more likely to toss like a wild bull in a net'.

They had now moved into the City, to a house in Coleman's Buildings. She seldom appeared downstairs. In the fifteen months remaining she spent much time studying and marking her Bible and her copy of the Olney hymns, and such hours as he could spare from his duties he spent in her room, the old ardour unquenched on either side. In private, he carefully prepared his spirit for the break.

Near the end she appeared to abandon her faith and to turn against her John. Newton was thrown into agony of

178

spirit, yet he showed himself ahead of his time in dealing with this, for he steadfastly refused to believe it to be caused by anything but a turn in her physical condition. After a fortnight her love to God and to John returned in full measure and continued unabated despite much suffering until, in the last days of 1790, after nearly forty years of marriage, the end came.

He described it to a friend a few months later: 'From about the month of August we were constrained to give up all hopes of her recovery. The Lord wonderfully preserved her from very severe pain – but she was in many respects a great sufferer though she would not readily own it, for she was favoured with exemplary and extraordinary patience. On 15th December the Lord released her from all her sorrows. I was watching over her with a candle in my hand and saw her draw her last breath.'

He insisted on preaching the next Sunday, saying, 'Dr. Pulpit is my best physician.' And he preached at her funeral, from a text, Habakkuk 3:17, 18, which he had reserved, unused, for the day of his greatest affliction, should he outlive her: 'Although the fig-tree shall not blossom, neither shall fruit be in the vine: the labour of the olive shall fail, and the fields shall yield no meat: the flock shall be cut off from the fold, and there shall be no herd in the stalls: yet I will rejoice in the Lord, I will joy in the God of my salvation.' *

When he came to speak of his wife, with a voice rather tremulous at first, he said he would like to mention candidly a few of her faults. 'He then spoke,' records one of the congregation, 'of her excessive attachment to himself – of her judging and estimating others with regard to himself, etc., which had the effect (though in the simplicity of his character he meant it not so) of leading his hearers to think

* Cowper had turned this text into the last verse of one of the loveliest of his Olney hymns, *Sometimes a light surprises*.

and ask, "If these were her chief faults, what were her excellences?" '

He published an artless account of her last days, and on the next 15 December, and for the four years following, he sent his friends an Anniversary poem and then ceased, saying that 'the Lord had healed the wound He made'. 'He has so indeed,' he told Wilberforce in 1797. 'I can say from my heart, He has done all things well. But the *scar* remains. She is still almost continuously present to my waking thoughts . . . But the Lord is good. And tho' I have often foolishly thought that if the Desire of my eyes should be taken from me, the sun would shine, *to me*, in vain, I believe taking all things together I have been more comfortable since she left me than I was before.'

He survived Polly seventeen years, almost to the day. During this time he helped to found the London Missionary Society and the equally worldwide Church Missionary Society, thankful that they would take the gospel to those parts of Africa where he had committed his crimes, as he now saw them, of enslaving God's children and carrying them to misery and death in distant lands. He was also a founder of the British and Foreign Bible Society, progenitor of countless Bible societies around the world.

Polly's niece, their adopted daughter Betsy Catlett, kept house for him until 1801, when he was in his seventy-sixth year. Then she went mad and had to be confined in Bedlam. Newton was almost overwhelmed. His eyesight was failing, so each day a maidservant or friend would lead him to Bethlehem Hospital (Bedlam's proper name) and he would stand outside her window until told that she had waved her handkerchief; he walked slowly back, content that she knew his love for her did not fail. After a year Betsy recovered, married an optician and the three lived together at Coleman's Buildings: Betsy read to him, guided him when he walked, cut up his food and watched his every need.

He grew deaf and almost wholly blind as his eightieth

year approached but he went on preaching. If he had been too inclined, when younger and over-busy, to think up his sermon between his house and his church, the increase of infirmity made his sermons even more discursive and ill planned. Yet his extraordinary perception of Scripture and of spiritual truth allowed his hearers to forget the defects. 'A most touching sermon,' wrote Elizabeth Fry's sister Catherine after attending 'old Newton's church' when in spiritual trouble. 'I can never forget the enjoyment and encouragement of that evening, and the delight of the whole church service on that occasion. It was what I wanted.'

His friends grew concerned at his increasing physical weakness and lapses of memory, the occasional bouts of depression which Newton attributed purely to old age, and his confusions in the pulpit. Richard Cecil ventured to suggest that perhaps he had better stop preaching. 'What!' exclaimed blind Newton when the suggestion penetrated his deafness. Raising his voice he shouted, 'Shall the old African blasphemer stop while he can speak?'

His Olney friend William Bull heard him ramble for fifty minutes on the words of Jesus: 'I, if I be lifted up from the earth will draw all men unto me.' Newton's understanding was in ruins, Bull reported, 'yet its ruins are precious, and the bits you pick up retain their intrinsic value, beauty and richness.'

In October 1806, when the nation celebrated the first anniversary of the Battle of Trafalgar, John Newton, aged eighty-one, was led to his pulpit to preach at a charity service to raise funds for the widows and wounded. The former midshipman sailed gallantly into action, all blindness and deafness ignored, but after a while he forgot what he was supposed to be preaching about, and paused. His curate had to mount the pulpit steps to remind him.

After that, he preached no more. Five months later in March 1807 Wilberforce's hard, long campaign achieved victory when Parliament abolished the British slave trade.

For Newton it was yet another amazing grace that he should live to see Abolition; just as Wilberforce, twenty-six years afterwards, heard on his death-bed that slavery itself had been abolished throughout the British Empire.

Newton lingered until four days before Christmas 1807, 'packed and sealed,' as he quipped, 'and waiting for the post.'

He was hardly able to speak. William Jay leaned over the bed to catch his last words.

Newton whispered: 'My memory is nearly gone. But I remember two things: That I am a great sinner . . .'

He paused for breath. '. . . And that Christ — *is a great Saviour*!'

Sources

MANUSCRIPTS

Bull MSS: letters, diaries etc. of John Newton and his wife in the possession of Miss Catherine Bull of Newport Pagnell, Buckinghamshire, a descendant of Newton's friend and executor, the Rev. William Bull.

Olney MSS: Newton letters etc. and especially the manuscript pages in his specially bound interleaved copy of *Letters to a Wife*, at the Cowper-Newton Museum, Olney.

Public Record Office MSS: Logs and Muster Book of H.M.S. *Harwich*.

Ridley Hall, Cambridge MSS: Newton's letters to John Thornton.

William's Library MSS: Newton's letters to Dr. David Jennings, at Dr. Williams's Library, Gordon Square, London W.C.1.

PRINTED WORKS BY JOHN NEWTON (*not* a complete list)

An Authentic Narrative 1764

Olney Hymns (and preface) 1779

Cardiphonia 1781

Thoughts upon the Slave Trade 1788

The Christian Correspondent: letters to Captain Alexander Clunie 1790

Letters to A Wife 1793

Memoirs of the Rev. W. Grimshaw 1797

Journal of A Slave Trader 1750–1754, edited, with an introduction, by Bernard Martin and Mark Spurrell 1962

OTHER WORKS

Bull, Josiah, *John Newton*: An Autobiography and Narrative, with unpublished diary extracts 1868

Bull, Josiah, *Memorials of the Rev. William Bull* 1864

Cecil, Richard, *Memoirs of the Rev. John Newton* 1808 (includes autobiographical fragment by Newton)

Jay, William, *Autobiography* 1854

King, James, and Ryskamp, Charles (eds.) *The Letters and Prose Writings of William Cowper*, Vol. I, 1750–1781 1979

Leaver, Robin A., *Olney Hymns 1779*, two articles in *Churchman*, 1979 (4) and 1980 (1)

Martin, Bernard, *John Newton*, 1950 (revised paperback edition, *An Ancient Mariner* 1960)

Stanhope, George, *The Christian's Pattern* 1708 (a translation of Thomas à Kempis, *De Imitatione Christi*)

Shaftesbury, 3rd Earl of, *Characteristicks* 1711

Wright, Thomas, *The Life of William Cowper* 2nd edition, 1921

The Correspondence of William Cowper 4 vols. 1904

Index

Biographies available from Kingsway by JOHN POLLOCK

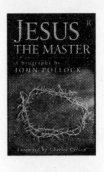

Jesus: the Master

A skilfully written yet simple, gripping story of Jesus, as seen through the eyes of the disciple John. In these pages you will meet Jesus in all of his humanity and all of his deity.

Paul: the Apostle

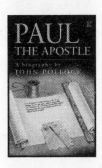

To discover the man behind New Testament writings, John Pollock travelled the roads Paul once walked. The result is a historically authentic picture of Paul which captures the drama and significance of his life.

Wesley: the Preacher

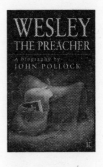

This popular biography provides a vivid picture of the spiritual journey of a man who had such an impact on eighteenth-century Britain and whose influence is still felt today.

Whitefield: the Evangelist

George Whitefield was a controversial but outstanding preacher who was the first major Christian leader to cross the Atlantic. Barred from church pulpits by scandalized clergy, he took to the open air where thousands gladly flocked to hear him. John Pollock tells the story of the man who in many ways started the work that Wesley continued.

Kingsway Publications